THE STEP BY STEP ART OF

Découpage

THE STEP BY STEP ART OF
Découpage

Text and Designs by
CHERYL OWEN

Photography by
STEVE TANNER

SMITHMARK

CLB 4092
© 1995 CLB Publishing

This edition published in 1995 by
SMITHMARK Publishers, a division of
U.S. Media Holdings, Inc.,
16 East 32nd Street, New York NY
10016

SMITHMARK books are available for
bulk purchase for sales promotion and
premium use. For details write or call
the manager of special sales,
SMITHMARK Publishers, Inc.
16 East 32nd Street, New York,
NY 10016; (212) 532-6600

Produced by CLB Publishing
Godalming Business Centre
Woolsack Way, Godalming, Surrey, UK

ISBN 0-8317-4996-2

Printed in Singapore
10 9 8 7 6 5 4 3 2 1

Contents

Introduction

Découpage is an age-old craft, which in this innovative book has been given a refreshing, contemporary approach. Here we show how everyday objects can be transformed quickly and inexpensively with just paper, scissors, glue and varnish. Decoupage is derived from the French word **découpure**, which literally means 'cutting out'. Paper motifs are cut out and glued to your chosen surface. The traditional aim of découpage is to then create a completely smooth surface so that the paper has the effect of inlay. This is achieved by applying coats of varnish. The finished effect depends upon the number of coats of varnish that are applied to the model.

Equipment

Only very basic equipment is needed for découpage, much of which you probably possess already. For comfort and safety, work on a flat, clean surface keeping sharp implements, glues, paints and varnishes out of a child's reach.

For drawing and cutting
Découpage designs can be drawn onto **tracing paper** and used as a guide for positioning the paper motifs. A **propelling pencil** or sharpened **HB pencil** is best for drawing. For accuracy, always use a **ruler** and **set square** when drawing squares and rectangles.

Small, sharp pointed **scissors** are indispensable for cutting out the motifs. **Embroidery, dissecting** or **manicure scissors** are ideal. Curved **nail scissors** are useful for cutting curves. Small, internal areas are best cut with a **craft knife**. Always use craft knives on a cutting mat and replace the blades often, since a blunt blade will tear the paper. Use a craft knife against a **metal ruler** when cutting straight lines.

For painting and varnishing
Most papers are liable to stretch when a water-based adhesive such as PVA medium is applied. This can cause problems if the cut paper motif is large. To prevent stretching, apply a coat of **sanding sealer** (available from art and do-it-yourself stores) to both sides of the paper before cutting. Apply sanding sealer to tissue paper and other fine papers before cutting. Sanding sealer can be used to prepare wooden surfaces too.

Sand wooden surfaces with **sandpaper** to prepare them for painting. Also key the painted surface with fine sandpaper between coats. When a number of coats of varnish have been applied, lightly sand with **glasspaper**.

A natural **sponge** can be used to dab on paint for a softened effect. Apply PVA medium with a flat paintbrush. For varnishing, a **badger-hair varnishing brush** is best, but a smaller flat paintbrush is easier to control when varnishing small items or intricate corners.

Use a **hairdryer** to apply warmth to a project that you are crackle glazing.

For sticking
Low-tack **masking tape** and **plastic putty** are used to hold paper motifs in place when you are arranging them. Always test the tape on a scrap of paper to make sure that the paper will not be damaged when the tape is removed.

PVA (polyvinyl acetate) medium is a non-toxic white solution that dries to a clear finish. The paper motifs are stuck in place with the medium. Keep kitchen paper towel close at hand to wipe off any excess glue.

Spray adhesive can be used to stick down paper motifs only if they are not to be varnished afterwards. Spray in a well-ventilated room.

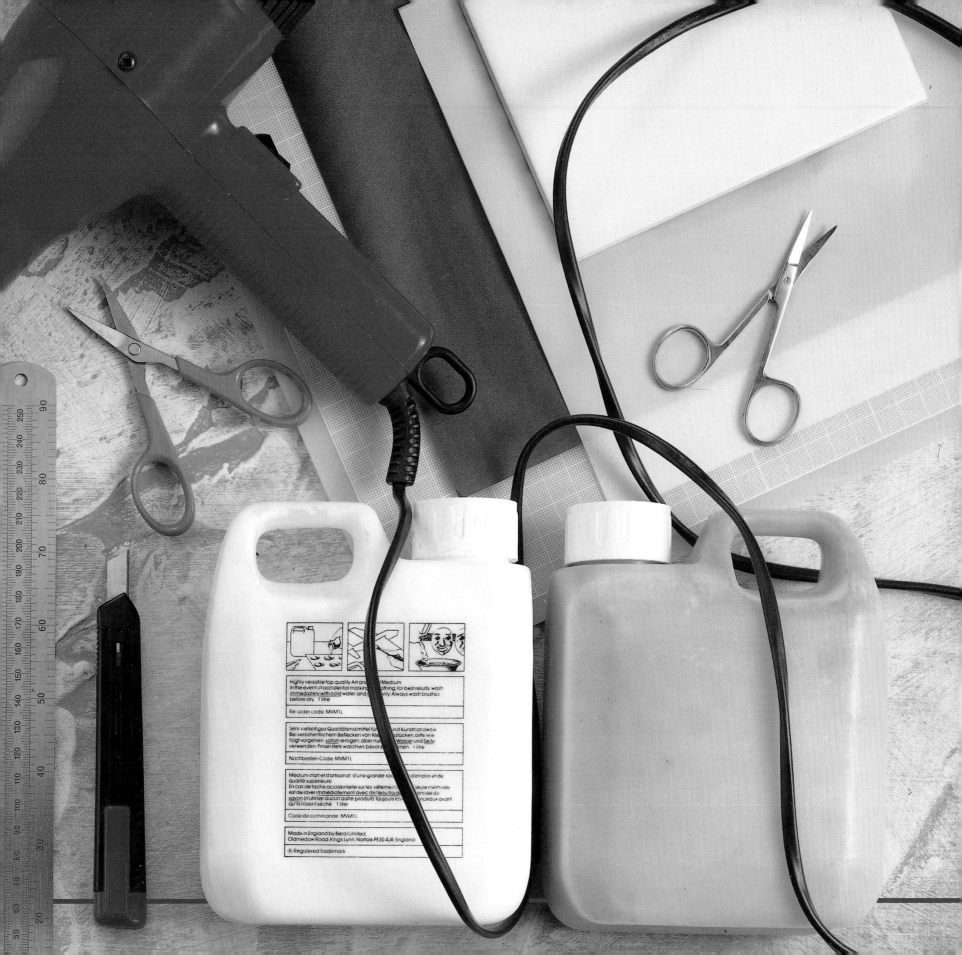

Materials

Items to découpage

Wood, metal, glass, ceramic and card can all be successfully découpaged. Small items of jewellery to full-sized furniture can benefit from all manner of pictorial or abstract designs.

Do not worry if your item to be decorated is scruffy, a coat of paint will give it a new lease of life. Often the used and worn look of old wood or metal gives character to the piece. The use of crackle glaze, an ageing medium, will give an additional antique quality to your work.

Papers

Traditionally, designs printed on white paper, often of botanical drawings, were hand coloured and then cut out to use for découpage. Many of these designs are reproduced in copyright-free books, which are available at book shops and art and craft stores. These designs can be photocopied and used again and again. They can also be reduced or enlarged to suit the size of the item they are to embellish. At a photocopy shop, experiment by photocopying black and white designs onto coloured papers, or by photocopying with a coloured ink. Colourful images can also be photocopied with a full-colour copier.

*The Victorians favoured using '**scraps**' for découpage. These are colourful printed motifs which are now reproduced and available from museums and craft stores. The motifs are cut out and often applied with edges overlapping so that the entire surface is covered.*

***Giftwrap** is an obvious choice for découpage. The huge range of colourful and inexpensive giftwrap available today makes it possible to decorate goods in a wide range of styles.*

*Good quality **magazines** and **brochures** also provide an inspiring source of pictures. Always make sure the reverse side does not show through by applying varnish to the right side. Photographic images from magazines are very effective when cut into squares to make mosaic pictures.*

Look beyond printed papers for a contemporary approach to découpage. **Plain coloured, marbled** and **tissue papers** can be cut into interesting shapes or torn for a free effect. Realistic **wood effect papers** are ideal for imitating marquetry.

Foil sweet papers, paper doilies and even **fine metals** are unusual materials to use but they do give stunning results. Do not overlook **fabric** as a material for découpage. The pliable nature of fabric is especially suitable for use on wicker furniture and accessories.

Motifs cut from **wallpaper** or **wallpaper borders** can be découpaged to co-ordinate the decor of your home, although the thickness of the paper will be apparent when varnished.

Paints and varnishes

Wooden surfaces to be découpaged can be painted or stained first if you wish. Sand wood lightly before painting. Apply **undercoat** or **primer** to wood first if you want to apply an even covering of paint. Use standard household paints when painting furniture.

Craft paints are very versatile, the colours mix well, dry quickly and most are non-toxic. Use oil paints to rub into the cracks of a piece that has been crackle glazed.

Spray paints give an even, professional finish and are very effective on metal. They should be used in a well-ventilated room, with the surrounding area protected by lots of newspaper.

Black and white photocopies can be coloured with **Indian inks** once they are stuck in position. Seal the photocopies with sanding sealer before gluing to protect the surface.

Water or **oil-based varnishes** are used to complete the découpage. These are available in gloss, satin (semi-gloss) and matt finishes. Gloss is the most hard-wearing finish and matt the least. For a durable matt finish, varnish with gloss varnish first and finish with two coats of matt varnish.

Water-based varnish dries quickly to a clear finish. Polyurethane oil-based varnishes take longer to dry and have a yellowing finish, which is effective if you want an antique feel to the piece. Oil-based varnish can be coloured with a little oil paint if you wish to tint the overall colouring.

Techniques

The same basic techniques are involved in most of the projects. Before you start any design, read the techniques described in this section. It is also helpful to study the photographs of the finished projects and to read through the accompanying step-by-step instructions before you begin.

Colourwashing

Plain wooden articles given a wash of colour provide an excellent background for découpage. Thin emulsion or craft paints with water on a ceramic tile or an old plate. Paint the solution onto the surface – two colours blended together on the wood looks very effective. Leave to dry.

Sponging paint

The application of paint with a sponge is a very simple way of producing an interesting effect. Brush a thin film of paint onto a ceramic tile or an old plate. Dab at the paint lightly with a dampened natural sponge, taking care not to pick up too much paint or the result will be too dense. Dab the paint at random onto the model.

Cutting

1 Roughly cut out your chosen motif so that it is easier to handle. Using small manicure, dissecting or embroidery scissors, cut out the design. Angle the lower blade toward the paper to avoid a stark white edge being visible around your cut motif.

2 Delicate extending parts of the motif can be joined with 'bridges' to support the cut shape until they are ready to be stuck in place. Cut off any fine lines. It is easier to cut any internal areas with a craft knife on a cutting mat.

Arranging motifs

Experiment with the positioning of the motifs. If the surface to be decorated is not horizontal, stick the pieces in place with plastic putty or a low-tack masking tape. Do not press the tape on firmly or it may remove the print when removed. If you are uncertain about the resulting layout, set the piece aside for a few days and then look at it afresh – you may see a solution or decide to start again.

Gluing

1 It is very important that the paper is completely stuck to the surface underneath, otherwise air bubbles will be trapped within the design, or varnish may seep under any unstuck edges. A plastic carrier bag, cut open and laid flat, is a practical surface to glue on. Use a flat paintbrush to brush the glue outwards from the centre. PVA medium can be thinned with a little water if you prefer, but do not thin it if using on glass or china.

2 Place the motif in position. Cut off any bridges at this point. If you are sticking motifs to a curved surface, cut into the design, preferably along any design lines so that the paper lays smoothly. Press smoothly outwards from the centre with your fingers, using kitchen paper towel to soak up any glue that seeps out from the edges. After a few minutes, run a finger nail around the outer edges to make sure they are stuck down.

15

Painting details

Once the motifs are stuck down, use a fine paintbrush to paint on any fine lines that were cut off. Use ceramic paints on glass or china.

Varnishing

1 *The end result of your découpaged model depends upon how many coats of varnish are applied. Apply the varnish in as dust-free an environment as possible. Stir the varnish thoroughly but slowly so that bubbles do not occur. Dip the lower third of a varnishing brush into the varnish. Starting at the centre, brush the varnish outwards, holding the brush at a low angle and working in one direction at a time. Check that there are no drips of varnish, then set aside to dry. Placing the model in an open box will help prevent fluff sticking to the varnish.*

2 *Continue applying coats of varnish, each time in a different direction to the last. The projects in this book have been given at least ten coats of varnish. This does not give a completely smooth surface, the paper motifs can still be felt slightly raised above the surface, but they have an attractive embossed feel. After eight coats of varnish, lightly sand the piece with glasspaper, then sand again between each subsequent coat of varnish. This helps the varnish to adhere and reduces the thickness of the varnish covering the paper motif.*

Crackle glaze

1 Crackle glaze is used to give an antique finish to a découpaged model. Several varieties are available at art and craft stores, each varying in technique depending upon the make, but the principle is the same. These instructions are only a guide, always refer to the manufacturer's directions and experiment first as many factors will influence the result. First, apply a coat of oil-based crackle glaze sparingly over at least eight coats of varnish. Leave until almost dry, usually two to four hours. The surface should feel dry but tacky.

2 Next, apply the water-based crackle glaze, usually a liquid gum arabic solution. If this coat is applied thinly, the cracks will be close together, if the coat is quite thick it will take longer to dry and the cracks will be wide and further apart. Leave for five minutes, then smooth over any visible brush marks with your fingers. Leave for at least one hour, then apply warmth by placing the model beside a radiator or heating it with a hairdryer. Cracks should then appear. Do not hold the hairdryer too close or the glaze will wrinkle.

3 Rub oil paint in a circular motion into the cracks with a kitchen towel. Wipe off the surplus, leaving the paint in the cracks. Set aside to dry overnight, then coat with polyurethane varnish to seal the crackle glaze.

Creative Containers

Here is a delightfully eclectic collection of
containers and boxes for all manner of practical
purposes or to hold treasures and keepsakes. Many
of the containers are pretty enough to be displayed
purely for decoration.

Creative Containers

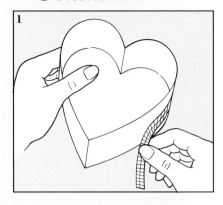

Cut out fruit and vegetable motifs from giftwrap or a wallpaper border. Arrange in place, remembering to create the designs with the lids on the boxes. Stick to the boxes following the gluing technique shown on page 15.

1 Cut a patterned edging strip from a wallpaper border and stick to the rim of a box.

2 Following the varnishing technique on page 16, varnish the boxes with a water-based varnish.

These Shaker style boxes, decorated with fruit and vegetable motifs cut from giftwrap, will add a country touch to any interior.

Creative Containers

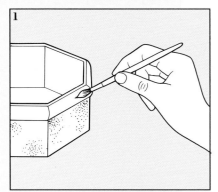

1 *Follow the colourwashing technique on page 14 to paint wooden wine bottle coasters and a bottle box. Sponge the coasters with gold craft paint following the sponging paint technique on page 14. Paint the rims gold. Thin gold craft paint with water and use it to paint the edges of the bottle box.*

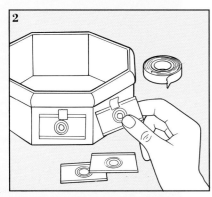

2 *For the coasters, cut out motifs from giftwrap. Refer to the arranging motifs technique on page 15 to position the motifs on the coasters. Wide strips of giftwrap were cut into sections and positioned on each hexagonal side. A head or glove motif and a narrow strip were applied to each hexagonal side of the green coaster.*

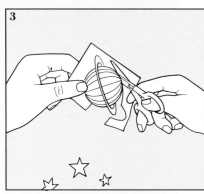

3 *Cut out motifs from giftwrap for the bottle box. Place the bottles in the box and arrange the motifs where they will be visible between the bottles and on the front and sides of the box. Stick in place with masking tape. Place small stars at random in any small gaps. Remove the bottles.*

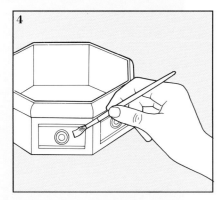

4 *Glue and varnish the pieces with water-based satin varnish following the gluing and varnishing techniques on pages 15–16. The bottle box was crackle glazed, then gold wax, available at art stores, was rubbed into the cracks (see page 17).*

▶ *Mythical gods and a galaxy of stars and planets decorate a bottle box and wine bottle coasters. The rich colours are highlighted with touches of gold.*

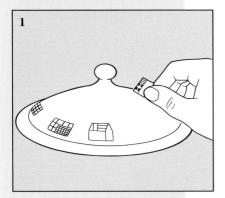

1 *The large blue canister has motifs cut from a giftwrap printed with patchwork quilt pictures. The central picture has been bordered with patchworked strips, and patchwork squares edge the lid. Uneven strips and squares cut from coloured papers will give a similar effect when co-ordinated with a naive picture. Apply the pieces following the arranging motifs, gluing and varnishing techniques on pages 15–16.*

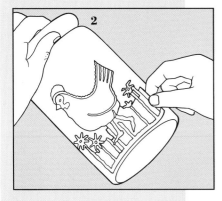

2 *The hen design on the pale blue canister has been cut from a giftwrap printed with rag rugs. First, paint a wooden canister with pale blue craft paint following the colourwashing technique on page 14. Allow the wood grain to show through the paint. Stick your main motif to the front and smaller motifs such as the flowers to the lid following the gluing and varnishing techniques on pages 15–16.*

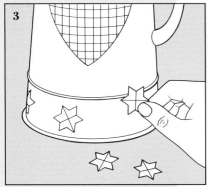

3 *Gingham papers decorate the yellow enamel coffee pot, although any simple all-over repeat design giftwrap will do. Cut out a large heart for the front and small stars for a border. Use stars and hearts to decorate the lid. Découpage the pot, following the gluing and varnishing techniques on pages 15–16.*

4 *The small white canister is decorated with hearts cut from giftwrap. Either use a giftwrap already printed with hearts or cut out heart shapes from coloured papers. Glue the hearts onto the pot, then varnish with water-based matt varnish following the gluing and varnishing techniques on pages 15–16.*

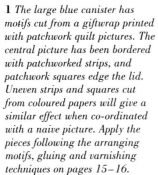

These practical kitchen canisters, decorated with simple Folk Art motifs, will give a warm, homespun look to a kitchen.

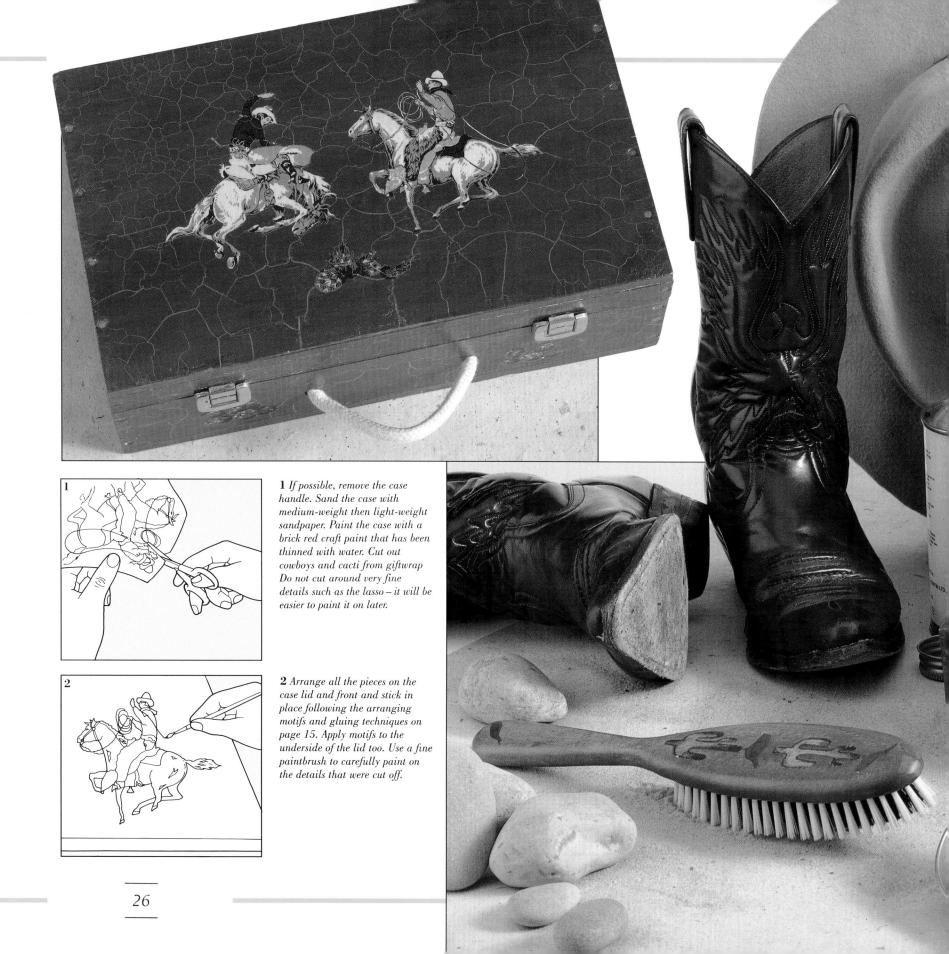

1 *If possible, remove the case handle. Sand the case with medium-weight then light-weight sandpaper. Paint the case with a brick red craft paint that has been thinned with water. Cut out cowboys and cacti from giftwrap Do not cut around very fine details such as the lasso – it will be easier to paint it on later.*

2 *Arrange all the pieces on the case lid and front and stick in place following the arranging motifs and gluing techniques on page 15. Apply motifs to the underside of the lid too. Use a fine paintbrush to carefully paint on the details that were cut off.*

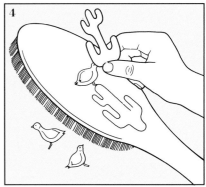

3 Varnish the case with water-based matt varnish following the varnishing technique on page 16. The outside of the case was crackle glazed and white oil paint was rubbed into the cracks. See the crackle glazing technique on page 17.

4 To decorate a wooden clothes brush, paint the brush with blue craft paint thinned with water. Apply only one coat of the thinned paint. Cut cacti and small birds from giftwrap and arrange on the back of the brush with the birds 'standing' on the cacti. Place a single bird on the handle. Glue the pieces in place, then varnish with water-based satin varnish (see the gluing and varnishing techniques on pages 15–16).

◄ A wooden wine case has been transformed into a practical container for shoe polish and brushes. A clothes brush with découpaged cacti completes the Wild West look.

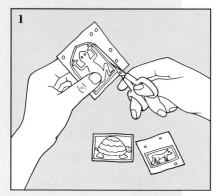

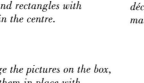

1 *To decorate the toy box, thin pink and mauve craft paints with water to paint the box following the colourwashing technique on page 14, allowing the colours to run together. Set aside to dry. Cut out motifs from giftwrap, here small framed natural history and animal motifs have been used. Alternatively, you can simply cut squares and rectangles with animals in the centre.*

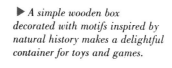

▶ *A simple wooden box decorated with motifs inspired by natural history makes a delightful container for toys and games.*

▼ *Trim a small wooden basket with colourful papers to hold sweets or tiny toys. Paint and découpage small wooden offcuts to make a set of fun building bricks.*

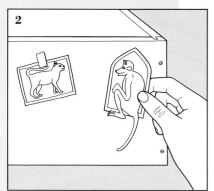

2 *Arrange the pictures on the box, sticking them in place with masking tape or plastic putty. Glue the pictures to the box following the gluing technique on page 15. Varnish with water-based matt varnish following the varnishing technique on page 16.*

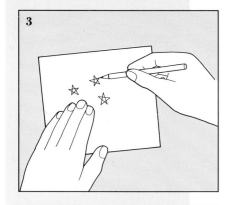

3 *To decorate a small wooden basket, cut triangles from various patterned giftwraps. Trim the edges to fit the top of the basket if necessary. Draw small stars on the back of giftwrap and cut out. Cut out chevrons for the handle.*

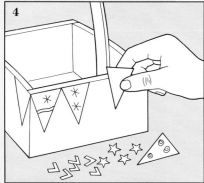

4 *Following the gluing technique on page 15, stick the triangles to the rim, with the stars stuck at random underneath. Stick the chevrons to the handle. Varnish the basket with water-based satin varnish following the varnishing technique on page 16. To make building bricks, saw offcuts of wood into cubes. Sand, then paint with craft paints. Follow the techniques on pages 15 – 16 to découpage with small motifs cut from giftwrap.*

Creative Containers

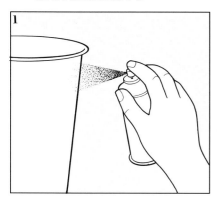

1 *Use a pair of pliers to remove the wire handle from a metal bucket. Spray paint the bucket and a metal watering can in bright colours.*

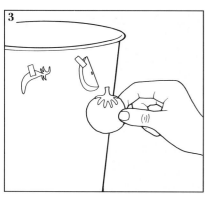

2 *To decorate the watering can, cut out flower heads from giftwrap. Sunflowers have been used in this example. Arrange the flowers around the watering can following the arranging motifs technique on page 15. Stick the flowers in place following the gluing technique on page 15. Stick one flower to the top of the can. Use a hole punch to punch holes in a co-ordinating coloured paper. Glue the punched circles in a border around the watering can and along the handle.*

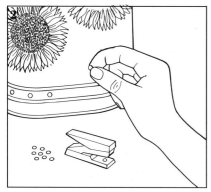

3 *To decorate the bucket, cut out gardening motifs from giftwrap. Arrange the pieces on the bucket at random following the arranging motifs technique on page 15. Stick down following the gluing technique on page 15.*

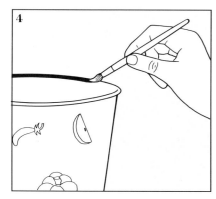

4 *Paint the bucket rim in a contrasting colour with enamel paint. Varnish the watering can and bucket with water-based gloss varnish following the varnishing technique on page 16. Paint the wooden handle for the bucket, then replace on the bucket.*

Creative
Containers

◀ *This colourful metal bucket and watering can, decorated with gardening motifs, would make a cheery addition to a conservatory.*

Creative Containers

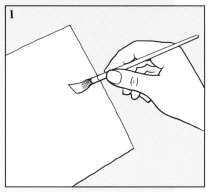

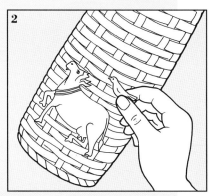

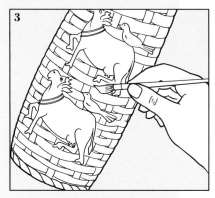

1 *Apply PVA medium to the back of the fabric to help prevent it from fraying. Leave to dry.*

2 *Cut out the fabric motifs and arrange on the wickerware. Stick in place following the gluing technique on page 15.*

3 *Apply ten coats of polyurethane satin varnish, allowing the varnish to dry between coats.*

◀ *As an alternative material to paper, fabric has been used to découpage this wicker case and covered bottle. The undulating surface of wickerware takes the draping qualities of these furnishing fabric motifs very well.*

33

Creative Containers

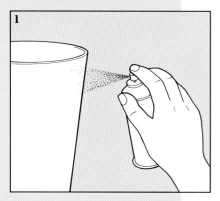

1 *Spray paint the waste bin with cream-coloured paint. Lightly spray the heraldic waste bin with mustard and yellow paint. Lightly spray the clock waste bin with silver and blue paint. Tear coloured tissue into irregular squares and rectangles. To strengthen the tissue, apply a coat of sanding sealer to both sides.*

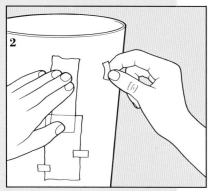

2 *Arrange the tissue pieces on the waste bins, overlapping the colour and sticking lightly in place with masking tape. Stick the tissue pieces in position following the gluing technique on page 15.*

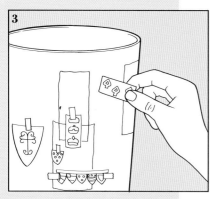

3 *Cut motifs from giftwrap. Heraldic shields, crowns and historic symbols were used for the heraldic waste bin – cut some of the motifs out neatly and others into an uneven square or rectangle. Clock faces were cut from giftwrap for the clock waste bin. Clock faces cut from magazine advertisements will also look very effective. Arrange the motifs on the waste bin, sticking them on lightly with masking tape.*

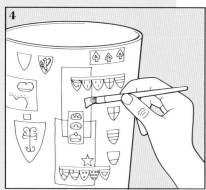

4 *When you are happy with the design, stick the pieces in position following the gluing technique on page 15. Varnish the waste bins following the varnishing technique on page 16 and using water-based matt varnish.*

▶ *Revamp old waste bins with spray paints, fine tissue papers and delicate paper motifs.*

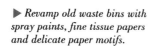

Glass and Glaze

Highlight the reflective qualities of glass with delicate and romantic images, or decorate brightly coloured ceramics with bold and flamboyant designs.

Glass and Glaze

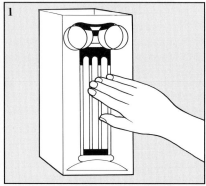

1 *To decorate the tall red vase, cut one motif from giftwrap large enough to fit the length of the vase – the ancient architectural column shown here was perfect. Stick in place following the gluing technique on page 15.*

2 *Drape some floral motifs cut from giftwrap around the column and lightly stick in place with masking tape. Glue in position. Glue various motifs to the other glass vessels. Varnish the glassware with water-based gloss varnish following the varnishing technique on page 16.*

Plain coloured glassware can be transformed into designer-style pieces with the application of various paper motifs.

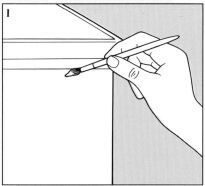

1 *Cut out 6 mm (¼ in) squares in plain colours from photographs in magazines. Apply PVA medium to one edge of a square ceramic planter. Stick the squares in a row along the edge. Continue around each side of each square.*

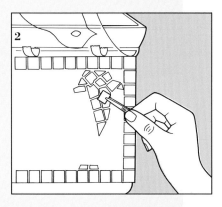

2 *To decorate a large planter with a picture on each side, draw a simple picture to fit within the mosaic frame on tracing paper. Stick the masking tape along the upper edge. Lift the tracing and spread a little PVA medium on the planter. Use tweezers to stick the squares on the planter, following the design of your tracing and replacing the tracing from time to time to check positioning. The squares can be trimmed to fit the required shape. Wipe off excess glue with kitchen paper towel.*

3 *Continue to fill in the picture. When the main pieces are in place, remove the tracing and fill in the background.*

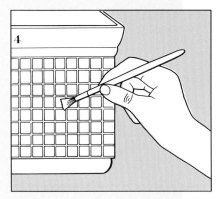

4 *To decorate a small planter in a simpler style, stick more squares in rows inside the mosaic frame in a contrasting colour. Fill in the frame with squares of different colours. Wipe off any excess glue as you work. Leave to dry, then varnish with water-based satin varnish following the varnishing technique on page 16.*

◄ *A mosaic of small squares cut
from photographs in magazines
decorates these attractive planters.*

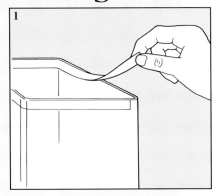

1 *To découpage the bowls, cut out large and small fish, shells, seahorses and other sea creatures from giftwrap. As a guide for positioning, stick a length of masking tape inside the top edge of the fish bowl to suggest the water level.*

This selection of glassware is inspired by the sea. The square fishbowl and the round bowl have paper motifs applied inside and are then painted within. A glass paperweight displaying a pair of proud seahorses completes the marine theme.

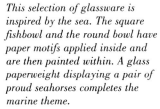

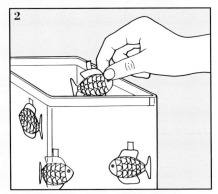

2 *Arrange the motifs inside the bowls, sticking them in place with a small strip of masking tape. Position the larger fish first in the fish bowl, adding seahorses and a shoal of smaller fish in the gaps. When you are happy with the design, remove one motif and paste the right side with PVA medium, spreading the medium outwards from the centre. Stick in place inside the bowl, smoothing the paper outwards from the centre. Wipe off any excess glue from the glass with a damp cloth. Stick the other motifs in place in the same way.*

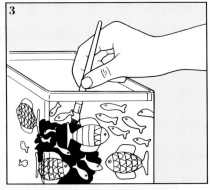

3 *Leave to dry for at least five hours. Check that all the edges are stuck down well. If they are not, apply PVA medium under the edge and stick down. Leave to dry. To paint the fish bowl, dab turquoise, green and blue ceramic paint inside the bowl, using a paintbrush and blending the colours together. Leave to dry, then peel off the masking tape.*

4 *To paint the round bowl after sticking on shell motifs, follow the sponging paint technique on page 14 to sponge red ceramic paint inside the bowl. Leave to dry, then dab yellow, orange and beige coloured ceramic paint inside the bowl with a paintbrush.*

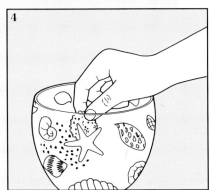

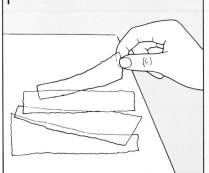

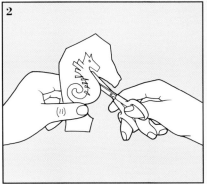

1 *For the paperweight, tear blue and turquoise tissue paper into strips. Spray with spray adhesive and stick to white paper, overlapping the edges of the tissue paper.*

2 *Cut the decorated paper to fit the recess of a glass paperweight. Cut out two seahorses from the giftwrap. Apply spray glue to the back of the seahorses and stick to the background paper. Draw around the paperweight onto a piece of sticky-backed plastic. Cut out, peel off the backing paper and carefully stick the decorated paper centrally on top. Stick under the paperweight.*

Glass and Glaze

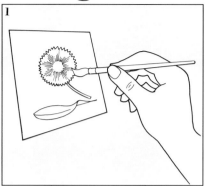

1 *To decorate the large green cup and saucer, photocopy botanical motifs from copyright-free source books, available from art and craft stores, onto coloured paper. Apply sanding sealer to both sides of the paper to protect the surface. Cut out the motifs, cutting off any fine details such as stems as these can be painted on later.*

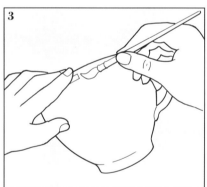

2 *Arrange the motifs on the cup and saucer and stick them lightly in place with masking tape. Refer to the gluing technique on page 15 to stick the pieces to the china, making cuts into the motif so that they lie flat over the curved surface. Paint in the fine details using ceramic paint.*

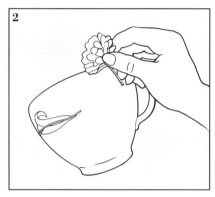

3 *To decorate the yellow mosaic cup and saucer, cut green and black coloured paper into strips approximately 8 mm (⁵⁄₁₆ in) wide. Cut the strips into squares and rectangles. Apply PVA medium to the top of a section of the cup and press green rectangles in a row onto the PVA medium. Continue sticking on the rectangles around the cup, wiping away the excess glue with a damp kitchen towel as you work.*

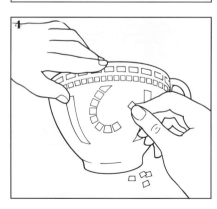

4 *Add a row of black squares below the green rectangles. Decorate the outer edge of the saucer in the same way. Measure the circumference of the cup with a tape measure and divide the cup into fifths with masking tape. Arrange black squares in a spiral design within one section. Stick in place with PVA medium, trimming the first and last square diagonally. Decorate the other sections in the same way. Remove the masking tape and glue a green square between each spiral.*

5 *Cut five 2 cm (¾ in) diameter circles of paper for templates and arrange equidistantly apart on the saucer. Stick black squares around each circle with PVA medium. Remove the templates. Stick a green square between each circle.*

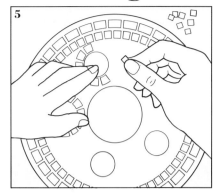

6 *To cover a small cup and saucer completely, cut out lots of 3 cm (1¼ in) diameter circles of green patterned giftwrap and magazine pictures. Stick the circles to the cup and saucer following the gluing technique on page 15, overlapping the circle edges so that the china is completely covered. Cut into the circles so that the paper lays flat.*

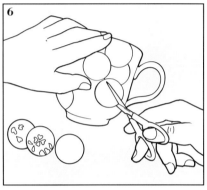

7 *Cut out cup shapes from yellow patterned paper giftwrap and magazine pictures. Stick around the cup and saucer.*

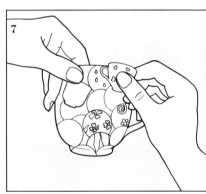

8 *Varnish the cups and saucers with water-based satin varnish following the varnishing technique on page 16.*

◀ *Découpaged cups and saucers will have pride of place in a pretty kitchen. Here are three different methods of decorating chinaware.*

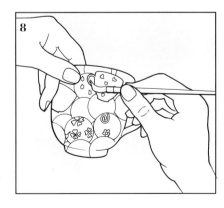

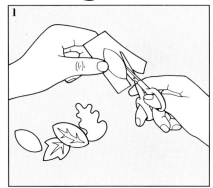

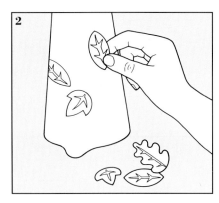

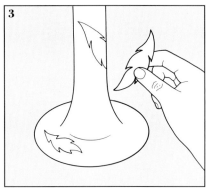

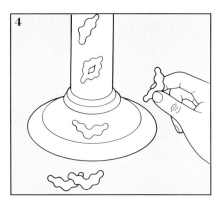

1 *To decorate the lamp base and shade, use the templates on pages 104–105 to cut leaves and flames from gold paper, cutting out the leaf veins. Cut enough flames to fit around the shade. The edges can be trimmed to adjust the size.*

2 *Follow the arranging motifs and gluing techniques on pages 14–15 to stick the leaves and flames in place. Varnish the lamp base with water-based satin varnish following the varnishing technique on page 16.*

3 *To decorate the tall ceramic candlesticks, use the templates on page 105 to cut feathers from gold and silver paper. Arrange at random on the candlesticks following the arranging motifs technique on page 14. Glue the feathers in position, then varnish them with water-based satin varnish following the gluing and varnishing techniques on pages 15–16.*

4 *To decorate the coloured glass candlestick, use the templates on page 105 to cut wedges, diamonds and boomerangs from two shades of gold paper. Cut out the cut-outs in the diamonds. Arrange the wedges and diamonds on the stem of the candlestick following the arranging motifs technique on page 14. Arrange the boomerangs in a border around the candlestick base.*

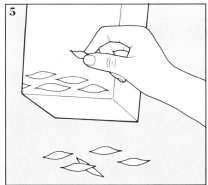

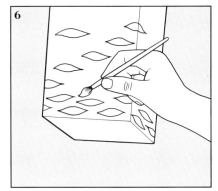

5 *Cut slivers of coloured papers to decorate the square candle holder. Arrange the pieces on one side of the candle holder, positioning them close together around the base and then further apart as you work toward the top.*

6 *Stick the pieces in place following the gluing technique on page 15. Work the other sides of the candle holder in the same way. Follow the varnishing technique on page 16 to varnish the candlesticks with water-based matt varnish.*

◀ *Ceramic and glass candlesticks and a lamp have been given an air of sophistication with stylized motifs cut from metallic papers.*

◀ Encircle a vibrant sun and moon with jaunty cut-outs for this pair of colourful decorative plates.

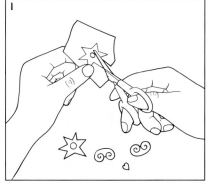

1 Cut out one or two large motifs for the plate centres and small motifs for the plate rims.

2 Arrange the pieces in position. Short strips of colourful patterns were arranged in a circle on the sun plate. Stick to the plate following the gluing technique shown on page 15.

3 Varnish the plate following the varnishing technique on page 16. Use water-based satin varnish.

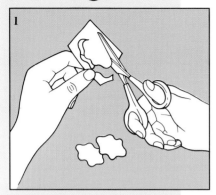

1 *To découpage the long dish, cut simple shapes from a sheet of thin copper (available at craft stores) using a pair of old scissors. Stick the shapes to a ceramic dish with strong glue.*

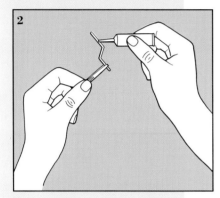

2 *Bend short lengths of wire into zig-zags. Holding the wire with a pair of tweezers, carefully run a line of strong glue along the wire. Use a gel glue as it is easier to control than in liquid form.*

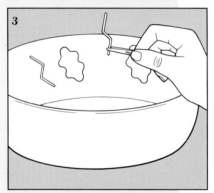

3 *Stick the wire to the dish between the copper shapes, using tweezers to position the pieces. Varnish the dish with ten coats of water-based matt varnish.*

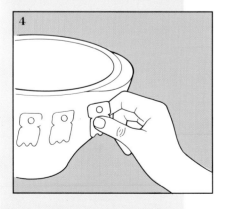

4 *Cut out a simple motif from coloured papers and stick in a row around a terracotta bowl following the gluing technique on page 15. Varnish the bowl with water-based satin varnish following the varnishing technique on page 16.*

◀ *A long ethnic style dish has been découpaged with fine metals as a contemporary alternative to paper. A South American motif decorates a terracotta bowl to give a rustic handcrafted effect.*

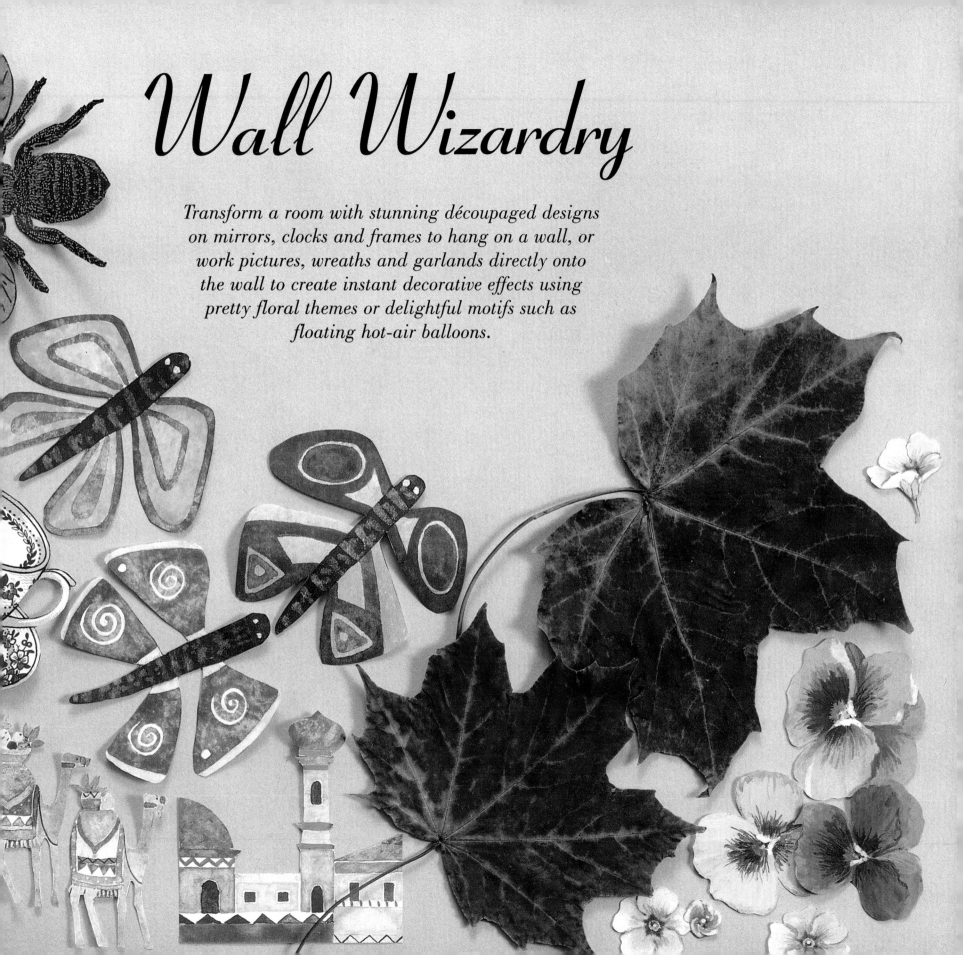

Wall Wizardry

Transform a room with stunning découpaged designs on mirrors, clocks and frames to hang on a wall, or work pictures, wreaths and garlands directly onto the wall to create instant decorative effects using pretty floral themes or delightful motifs such as floating hot-air balloons.

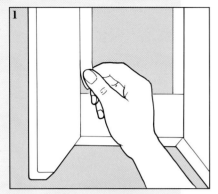

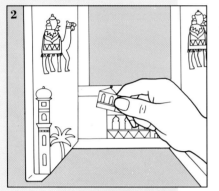

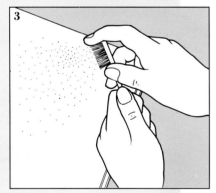

▶ *Frame a mirror with Arabic motifs to lend a Far Eastern flavour to a room.*

1 *To protect the glass on the mirror, apply strips of masking tape around the edges of the glass. Cut out camels, palm trees and moorish buildings from giftwrap. Arrange the camels and palm trees on the vertical sides of the frame and the buildings on the horizontal sides.*

2 *Stick the motifs in place following the gluing technique on page 15. Varnish the frame with water-based satin varnish following the varnishing technique on page 16. This frame has been crackle glazed with lemon oil paint rubbed into the cracks (see the crackle glazing technique on page 17).*

3 *To decorate a clock, paint a clock face and hands with craft paint. Clock faces, hands and clockworks are available from craft stores. To spatter paint on the clock face and hands, dab an old toothbrush with craft paint. Hold the brush at a 45° angle and run your finger through the bristles to distribute the paint at random. Gold, turquoise and blue paints were spattered onto this mauve painted clock face with gold paint spattered onto turquoise hands. If the clock face has a bevelled edge, a coloured strip can be painted around the edge.*

4 *Trace the clock face template on page 104. Cut the numerals from coloured paper or giftwrap. Tape the top of the tracing to the clock face, matching the centre. Stick the numerals to the clock following the gluing technique on page 15 and slipping the pieces under the tracing to position them correctly.*

5 *Cut out eight small motifs such as tiny circles. Slip these under the tracing and place at the dots to mark the remaining hour points. Carefully remove the tracing. Arrange four gold coin pendants along the lower edge. Cut out various motifs to decorate the clock. Arrange on the clock, placing one motif over the centre.*

6 *Remove any hour points that will be hidden by the other motifs. Stick all the pieces in place following the gluing technique on page 15. Tiny motifs can be stuck along the clock edges. Remove the coins. Cut out the centre hole through the central motif with a craft knife. Varnish the clock with water-based satin varnish following the varnishing technique on page 16. Assemble the clockwork following the manufacturer's instructions.*

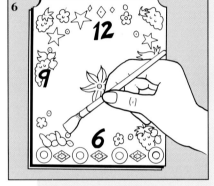

7 *To trim the lower edge with tassels, cut four skeins of pearlized stranded cotton embroidery threads into 12 cm (4¾ in) lengths. Put aside one length of each skein and bunch the remaining lengths together. Fold the single strand in half and place under the bunch. Pull the ends of the single strand through the folded loop, enclosing the bunched strands.*

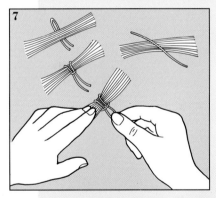

8 *Insert the single strand ends through the hole in a bell cap – a jewellery finding available at craft stores. Insert the thread ends through the hole in a gold coin pendant. Glue with strong adhesive to the back of the coin. Glue the coins to the lower edge of the clock with strong adhesive. Trim the tassel ends level.*

◄ *This flamboyant clock has been decorated with many colourful images. Jaunty hanging tassels complete the effect.*

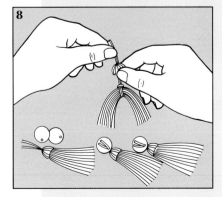

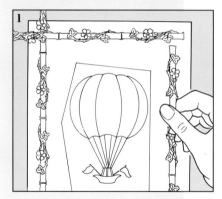

1 *The border surrounding the hot-air balloon and on the picture mount were photocopied from a copyright-free book of borders and ornaments. Photocopy the borders (so that you have four strips) and four ornaments for the picture mount corners. Coat both sides with sanding sealer. Colour the photocopies with coloured pencils and cut out. Roughly cut out a hot-air balloon from giftwrap and place on a sheet of tracing paper. Arrange the strips of the frame around the balloon.*

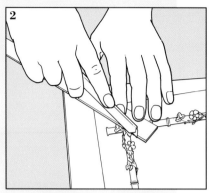

2 *Trace the picture mount onto tracing paper and arrange the strips on top. Draw the position of the strips onto the tracing paper, using a ruler and protractor so that the right angles are accurate. With the tracing paper on a cutting mat, re-arrange the strips accurately in place. Cut diagonally through the corners using a craft knife and protractor and cutting outwards from the inner corners.*

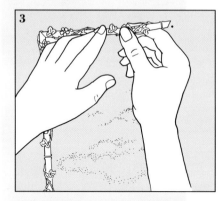

3 *Lightly tape the balloon frame tracing to a blue painted wall with masking tape. Mark the corners by lightly pressing in a nail point. Remove the tracing. Follow the sponging paint technique on page 14 to lightly sponge on 'clouds' with white paint, allowing the clouds to extend beyond the frame position. Leave to dry, then lightly sponge on silver craft paint under the clouds. Stick the borders to the wall between the corner points with wallpaper border paste.*

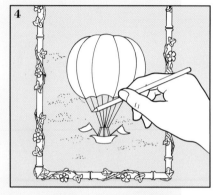

4 *Cut out the balloon, cutting through any fine ropes. Stick to the wall with wallpaper border paste. Add smaller balloons to the wall. Draw the ropes with a coloured pencil or fine pen. Place the border tracing on the picture mount and mark the outer corners with a pin. Remove the tracing. Stick the borders to the mount with spray adhesive. Stick the ornaments over the mitred joins.*

▶ *Create a tranquil scene of hot-air balloons floating through silver-lined clouds, or frame a favourite photograph with a bold hand-coloured border.*

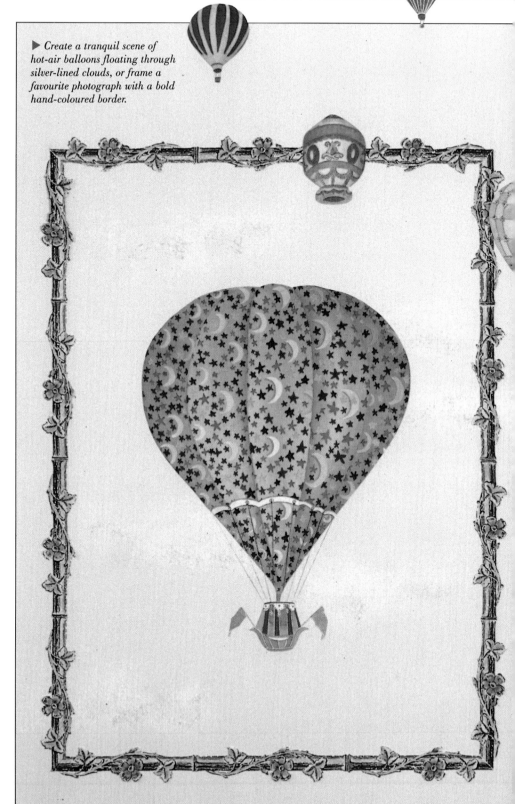

1 *Lightly draw lines on the wall where the shelves will be placed, use a spirit level to make the lines level. Stick teacups cut from giftwrap equidistant apart in a row along the lines, using wallpaper border paste. If you do not have a suitable giftwrap, cut out teacup and saucer shapes from coloured papers. Attach the shelves to the wall below the teacups.*

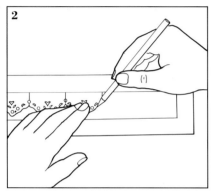

2 *To make the shelf edging, draw a 3.8 cm (1½ in) wide strip on white paper the length of the shelf. Refer to the template on page 107 to cut a shelf edging section from thick paper. Punch holes at the dots with a single hole punch. Cut around the cut-outs. Place on the wrong side of the strip with the upper edges level. Draw around the zig-zag edges, the cut-outs and holes. Move the template along and mark the design in the same way all along the strip.*

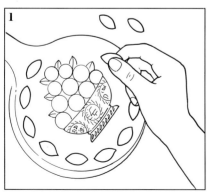

3 *Cut out the strip and cut-outs with a craft knife. Punch holes with a single hole punch. Fix the edging to the shelf edge with a panel pin at each end.*

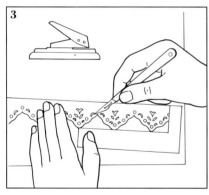

1 *To decorate the large sandwich board, refer to the colourwashing technique on page 14 to paint the back and edges of the board with blue and turquoise craft paints. Arrange butterflies and bugs cut from giftwrap on top. Paint the small board and edges blue. Leave to dry, then sponge with pale blue craft paint, following the sponging paint technique on page 14. Arrange a motif cut from giftwrap, such as this bowl of oranges, in the centre. Encircle with leaf shapes cut from green paper. Stick all the motifs in place following the gluing technique on page 15. Use a fine paintbrush to paint the antennae on the butterflies. Varnish with water-based satin varnish following the varnishing technique on page 16.*

This trompe l'oeil *of pretty china teacups sitting on shelves is created using teacups cut from giftwrap. Cut-work shelf edging completes the theme.*

▶ Decorate the back of wooden sandwich boards with découpaged motifs and suspend on ribbons.

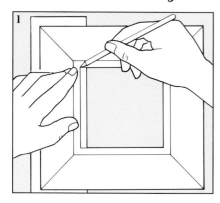

1 *To cover a picture frame with a map, first remove the glass and backing. Cut four strips from the map 3 cm (1¼ in) wider than the front panels of the frame. Lay the frame face down centrally on the wrong side of one strip. Mark the map at the inner and outer edges of the corners with a pencil.*

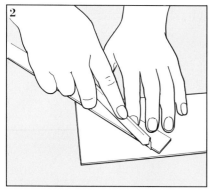

2 *Remove the frame. Join the marked points with a pencil. Starting at an inner corner, cut along the mitred lines with a craft knife, cutting to the outer edge of the paper.*

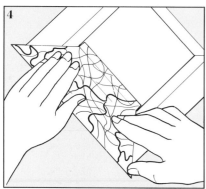

3 *Next, cut from an inner corner to the long edge at right angles to the long edges. Prepare the other strips for the other front panels in the same way.*

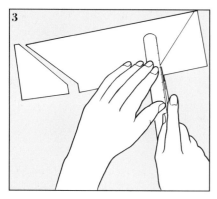

4 *Apply PVA medium to the back of one strip, lay the strip along one front panel of the frame, matching the position of the mitred corners. Press the paper in place, smoothing outwards from the centre.*

▶ *Revive holiday memories by framing souvenirs in map-covered picture frames. Small mementos of natural history excursions can be captured in box frames decorated with natural images.*

5 *Turn the long edges to the underside, snipping off the excess paper at the outer corners. Cover the other panels in the same way. Apply two coats of water-based matt varnish to protect the frame.*

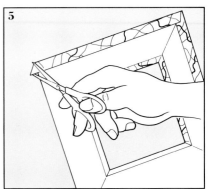

6 *Cut a square or rectangle of paper to fit inside the frame. Cut or tear a piece of paper in another colour and stick on top with spray adhesive. Arrange your display pieces on top then glue in place. Reassemble the frame.*

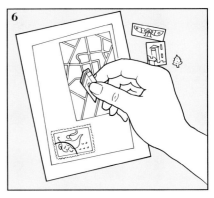

1 *Remove the glass and backing from a small box frame. Cut out motifs from giftwrap – here photographic images of natural materials were used. Arrange the motifs on the frame, allowing some to overlap the edges.*

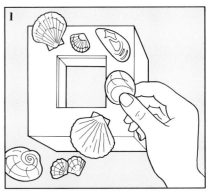

2 *When you are happy with the design, stick the motifs in place following the gluing technique on page 15. Take care to stick the motifs smoothly over the edges of the frame. Glue on some more motifs on the sides of the frame, sticking them over the edges and continuing the motifs onto the underside. Varnish the frames with water-based matt varnish following the varnishing technique on page 16.*

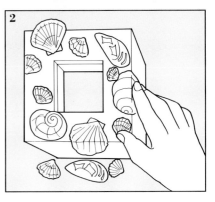

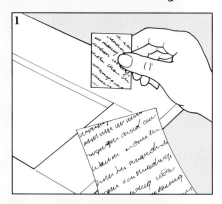

1 *Photocopy handwritten documents and old letters. Paint with sanding sealer to protect the surface. Cut the photocopies into strips and rectangles. Arrange the papers on the wooden components of a key cupboard kit. Place some pieces showing the wording upside down.*

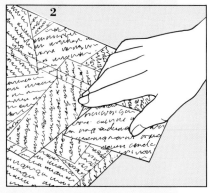

2 *When you are happy with the design, stick the papers in place following the gluing technique on page 15. Stick down the underlaying papers first, cutting into any intricate corners so that the paper lays flat. Stick offcuts of paper over any gaps.*

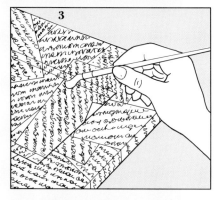

3 *Paint the backing board quickly and unevenly with burnt sienna and brick red Indian inks. Paint the other kit components with burnt sienna and sunshine yellow Indian inks. Leave to dry.*

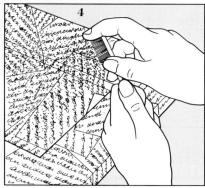

4 *Dab an old toothbrush into gol craft paint. Holding the brush at an angle, run your fingers through the bristles to distribute the paint at random over the kit pieces. Leave to dry, then assembl the kit. Paint the handle gold. D not attach the key hooks. Apply four coats of water-based satin varnish. Fix the hooks in place.*

▶ *A noble feeling of antiquity has been given to this key cupboard by covering it completely with photocopies of heirloom documents. The cupboard is then painted with Indian inks and highlighted with gold paint.*

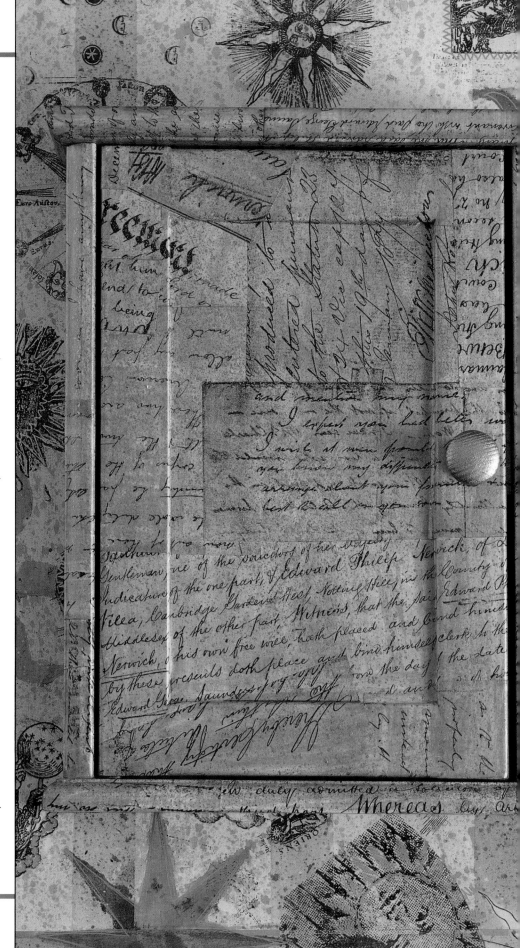

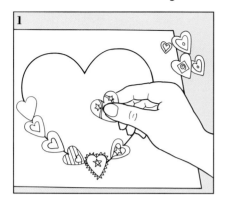

1 *To make a wreath, cut out motifs from giftwrap and arrange in a pleasing design on paper. A circle or heart can be drawn first on the paper as a guide to the shape of the wreath. Arrange the motifs singly as illustrated on the butterfly and large heart wreath, or overlap the pieces as on the other wreaths.*

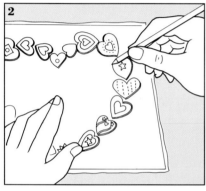

2 *To make a garland, draw a gentle curve on paper – half the length of your desired garland. Cut out motifs from giftwrap, such as the fruits displayed here, and arrange along the curve. Place tracing paper on top, or unroll a roll of greaseproof paper on top of the wreaths and garland. Trace around the outer and inner edges.*

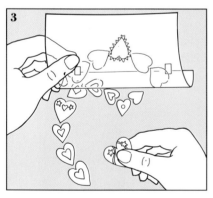

3 *Lightly tape the tracing to the wall with masking tape. Glue the motifs to the wall with wallpaper border paste following the gluing technique on page 15 and using the tracing as a guide for positioning the pieces. Work the other half of the garland in the same way. Stick down a large motif in the centre.*

4 *Paint any fine details, such as the butterfly antennae, onto the wall with acrylic paints.*

▶ *Pretty paper motifs make a wonderful display when applied to the wall of a plain room in the form of a garland or wreaths.*

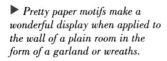

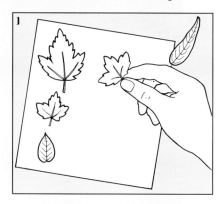

1 *To decorate a wooden shelf unit, gather together a collection of freshly fallen leaves. Either press the leaves in a flower press or slip the leaves between two sheets of kitchen paper towel and place within the pages of a heavy book. Leave for a few weeks.*

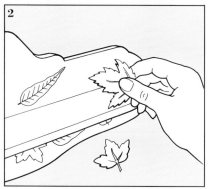

2 *Refer to the instructions on page 14 to colourwash the shelf unit in autumnal colours – here yellow and red were used. Arrange the leaves on the unit and stick in place. Varnish with water-based satin varnish following the gluing and varnishing techniques on pages 15–16.*

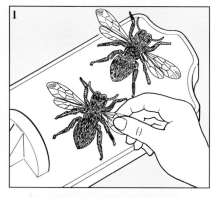

1 *Colour a wooden candle sconce with a wood stain or burnt umber acrylic paint thinned with water. Cut out bee motifs from giftwrap. These fine examples were printed on brown parcel paper. Arrange the bees on the sconce, allowing them to overlap the edges.*

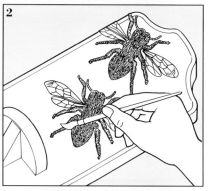

2 *Follow the instructions on page 15 to stick the bees to the sconce, cutting into the motifs so that they fit smoothly around any corners or curves. Varnish the sconce with water-based satin varnish following the varnishing technique on page 16.*

▶ *Capture the beauty of fallen autumn leaves with a découpaged shelf unit of pressed leaves. As a variation, pretty pressed flowers could be substituted to evoke a feeling of springtime all year round.*

▶ *A wooden candle sconce shows découpaged bee motifs hovering around an aromatic beeswax candle.*

Gifts Galore

*A handcrafted gift is always particularly special.
This chapter presents stylish ideas that you can
recreate for any occasion. There are practical presents
to entertain, like a colourful puppet theatre complete
with puppets, or a formal checkers board. Easy-to-make
greeting cards and giftwrap are included to give
a finishing touch to your creation.*

1 *For an urn of flowers, cut a 35 cm (14 in) square of textured apricot-coloured paper. Coat both sides with sanding sealer so that the paper is easier to handle. Leave to dry, then stick to one end of an A2 size sheet of mounting board with PVA medium.*

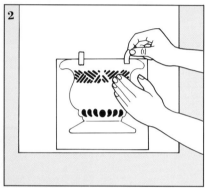

2 *Use the template on page 105 to trace and cut out an urn from tracing paper. Refer to the template to cut out the details from a darker shade of apricot paper. Place the template over the apricot square with the upper edges level. Lightly tape the upper edge in place with masking tape.*

3 *Lightly draw around the urn with a pencil. Glue the urn details in place with PVA medium, slipping the pieces under the tracing paper to position them correctly. Remove the tracing paper from the board.*

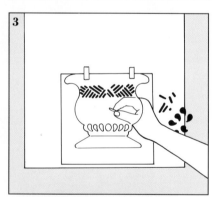

4 *Paint the mounting board above the urn with craft paints, mixing green and black together to make a dark green. Leave to dry. Cut out flowers and leaves from giftwrap. Arrange on the board above the urn, overlapping some flower edges but allowing the dark background to show in places. Arrange some pieces to overhang the urn. Place leaves and seed pods in any large gaps.*

▶ *Poppies and petunias overflow a regal urn to create a charming firescreen that will adorn your fireplace in the summer months.*

5 *When you are happy with the design, stick the pieces in place following the gluing technique on page 15 and sticking down the underlaying pieces first. Use a craft knife to cut around the outer edge of the urn and flowers. Paint the cut edges to match the urn and the dark green background above the urn.*

◄ ▼ *A pair of pecking hen dummy boards will lend a country feel to their surroundings and will amuse and delight your friends.*

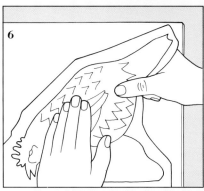

6 *To make a hen dummy board, choose a giftwrap with large motifs such as birds or animals. Roughly cut out the motif and coat both sides with sanding sealer. Stick to a piece of mounting board following the gluing technique on page 15. Cut out the image with a craft knife. Paint the cut edges black.*

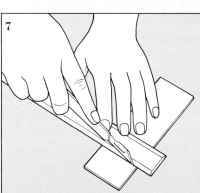

7 *Follow the varnishing technique on page 16 to varnish the firescreen with water-based matt varnish. Varnish the hen with two coats of water-based gloss varnish. Refer to the diagram on page 106 to cut a large stand for the firescreen and a small stand for the hen. Score along the line.*

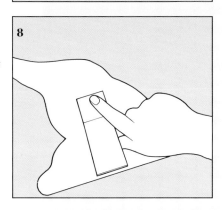

8 *Bend the tab backwards. Use all-purpose household glue to stick the tab to the back of the model, making sure that the tab is centred and that the lower edges of the tab and urn are level.*

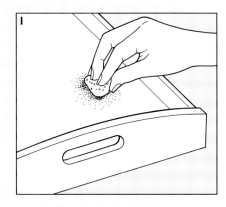

1 *Undercoat a wooden tray with acrylic gesso or emulsion paint. Paint the base with beige craft paint and leave to dry. Follow the sponging paint technique on page 14 to sponge the base with white and silver craft paint.*

▶ *This handsome tray is trimmed with elegant alphabetical letters. Apply the letters at random or spell out a heartfelt message.*

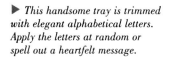

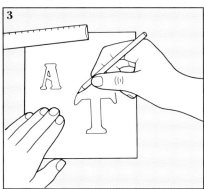

2 *Paint the sides and underside of the tray red, applying only one coat so that the paint surface appears patchy.*

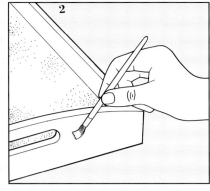

3 *Refer to the photograph or typefaces in magazines or copyright-free books to draw various letters on paper.*

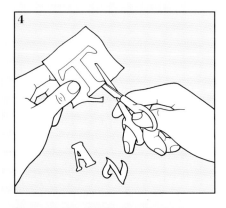

4 *Cut out the letters and use them as templates. With the wrong side uppermost, draw around the letters on the back of red and green marbled paper.*

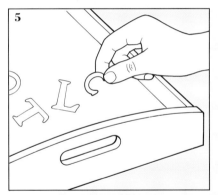

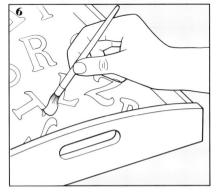

5 *Arrange the letters on the tray. Stick in position following the gluing technique on page 15.*

6 *Varnish the tray with water-based satin varnish following the varnishing technique on page 16. The sides and underside of the tray need only be varnished twice.*

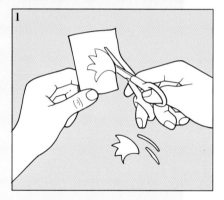

1 *To make a placemat, cut a rectangle of mounting board 33 x 24 cm (13 x 9½ in). Spray paint the mat. Choose four coloured papers in contrasting colours. Refer to the templates on page 106 to cut out two end panels, cutting either a matching pair or one panel freehand. Also cut eight flowers and eight veins or seeds from the papers.*

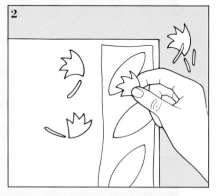

2 *Cut out the cut-outs on the end panels. Arrange the panels within the short ends of the mat. Arrange the flowers between the panels, placing a different coloured stem or pistil with each flower head.*

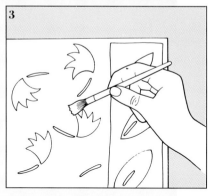

3 *When you are happy with the arrangement, stick all the pieces in place following the gluing technique on page 15. Stick the veins or seeds in the cut-outs. Varnish the mats following the varnishing technique on page 16 using water-based matt varnish.*

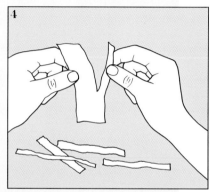

4 *Paint wooden napkin rings with craft paints. Coat both sides of coloured tissue paper with sanding sealer. Tear the tissue into strips when it has dried. Stick the strips in a criss-cross design on the napkin rings following the gluing technique on page 15, sticking the ends inside the ring.*

◀ *These bright and cheery placemats are influenced by floral textiles from the 1930s. A pair of napkin rings patterned with tissue papers continues the theme.*

5 *If the rings have a very curved shape, use short strips and overlap the ends to rejoin them.*

6 *Tear small squares or diamonds of tissue paper and stick in the gaps.*

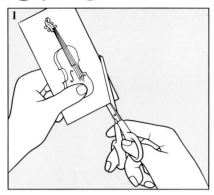

1 *Photocopy images from a copyright-free book onto coloured paper. Either cut out the images accurately or roughly cut out a rectangle or square with the image in the centre. Alternatively, tear the paper around the image.*

Stylish greeting cards and giftwrappings can be accomplished quickly and inexpensively by using images photocopied onto coloured papers.

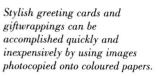

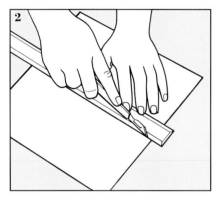

2 *Coloured card can be used to make the cards, or coloured paper can be applied to thin card with spray adhesive. Thick handmade paper was used for the torn-edged picture of an animal tamer. Cut a rectangle of coloured card or thick paper for the greeting cards, score across the centre and fold in half.*

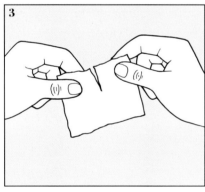

3 *Roughly tear a rectangle of coloured tissue for the violin card and handmade paper for the tiger card. Stick to the card front with spray adhesive.*

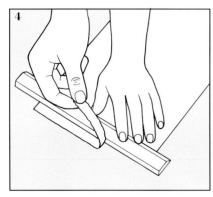

4 *To tear a rectangle of coloured paper accurately for the winged woman card, hold a ruler firmly on the paper. Lift the paper against the ruler to tear straight edges. Stick the rectangle diagonally on the card front with spray adhesive. Stick the image on top with spray adhesive. Stick the animal tamer picture to the card front with spray adhesive.*

5 *Stick photocopied motifs to coloured paper to use as giftwrapping, or stick to a gift box with spray adhesive.*

6 *For giftwrap, tear small squares of handmade paper and stick to gold paper at random with double-sided tape.*

▼ *Cut gift tags from coloured card. A torn rectangle of coloured paper can be applied with spray adhesive. Punch a hole at one end and thread with giftwrapping ribbon.*

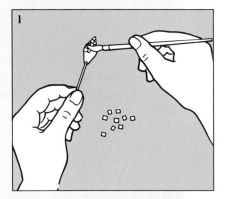

1 *Cut coloured paper into small squares or narrow strips. Slip beads onto cocktail sticks to make them easier to handle. Apply PVA medium to the beads or a small area of the box. Press on a square or strip. Coat with PVA medium then apply more squares or strips, overlapping the edges until the item is completely covered. Wrap the strips around a large ring-shaped pendant.*

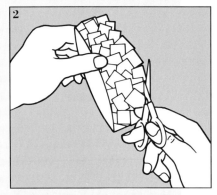

2 *Trim away the paper around the bead holes and edges of the box with a small pair of scissors. Paint the interior of the box gold. Cut small shapes from contrasting or co-ordinating coloured paper.*

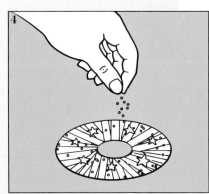

3 *Dab PVA medium on the item to be decorated and press on the shapes either at random as on the jewellery or in a pattern as on the box. Strips of coloured paper were stuck around the blue earrings. A large green star was stuck to the centre of the box, a large yellow circle was stuck on top of that with a smaller blue circle stuck down last.*

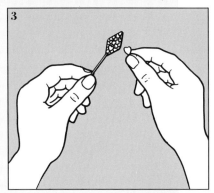

4 *Rub gold wax (available at art stores) sparingly over the jewellery and the box. To add sparkle to the pendant, apply PVA medium to the ring. Sprinkle sequin dust, which is the tiny holes cut from sequins, on top. Sequin dust is easily available at craft and specialist bead stores. Leave to dry, then shake off the excess. Varnish all the pieces with water-based satin varnish.*

Stunning beads and a matching box to contain them have been decorated with the same simple découpage technique to create these stylish pieces.

5 Use gold dimensional paint to outline the small shapes or to draw in patterns. Leave to dry. Craft and specialist bead stores sell findings to make up the jewellery. To make the hat pins, slip two beads onto a hat pin, add the découpaged bead, then a smaller bead. Dab strong glue onto the pin after the last bead. Slip another small bead onto the glue on the pin.

6 To make up the pink earrings, bend fine gold wire in a loop through the earring hole with pliers. Thread three beads onto the wire. Cut the wire 1 cm (⅜ in) above the last bead. Bend the wire into a loop and fix to a jumpring. Fix the jumpring to an earring wire.

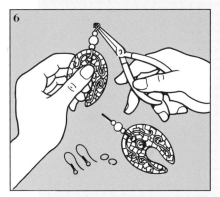

7 To make up the blue earrings, thread a small bead onto a headpin, then thread on the blue découpaged bead. Thread on two more small beads. Cut the wire 1 cm ⅜ in) above the last bead. Bend the wire into a loop with pliers. Fix to an earring wire.

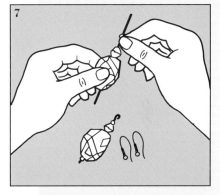

8 Bend a length of thronging in half, slip the folded loop through the pendant ring. Pull the thronging ends through the loop enclosing the ring. Thread on a bead, then knot the thronging against the bead. To make up the necklace, thread large découpaged beads onto thronging with flat beads in between and small beads at each side. Knot the pendant and necklace thronging and thread a bead onto each end. Knot the thronging ends.

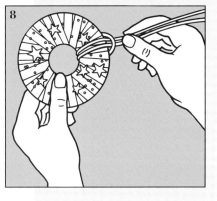

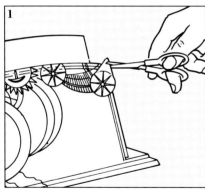

1 *To decorate a wooden letter rack, cut out nautical motifs from giftwrap and magazines. Follow the gluing technique on page 15 to stick the motifs to the rack, overlapping the edges until the rack is completely covered. Snip into the motifs so that they fit neatly around the corners and any curved edges.*

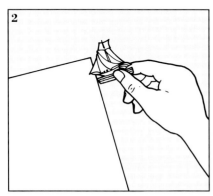

2 *Decorate a co-ordinating ruler by lightly sponging the ruler with gold craft paint, following the sponging paint technique on page 14. Cut out motifs from giftwrap, such as the fishes illustrated here, and stick to the ruler following the gluing technique on page 15. Varnish the letter rack and top of the ruler with water-based satin varnish following the varnishing technique on page 16. Stick motifs cut from giftwrap to sheets of writing paper and envelopes with spray adhesive.*

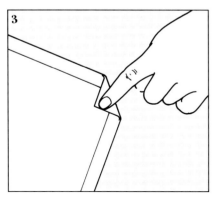

3 *To make the album, cut two rectangles of thick card 28 x 25 cm (11 x 10 in) for the covers. Cut two rectangles of coloured paper to cover the card rectangles 32 x 29 cm (12½ x 11½ in). Coat both sides of the paper with sanding sealer. Stick the card rectangles centrally on the papers with PVA medium. Stick the corners and then the edges of the paper over the card.*

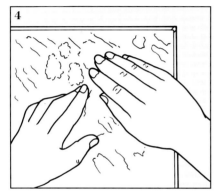

4 *Cut two rectangles of marbled paper and thirty rectangles of thick black paper 27 x 24 cm (10½ x 9½ in). Glue the marbled papers to the underside of the covers. Use a hole punch to punch a pair of holes on one short edge of each of the covers and each of the black pages. Stick a large motif cut from giftwrap to the top of one cover following the gluing technique on page 15. Sandwich the black pages between the covers, matching the holes. Fold a fine tassel-ended cord in half.*

5 *Thread the folded end down through the lower hole of the top cover, the pages and the back cover, then up again through the upper holes.*

◀ *Nautical images completely cover a letter rack. This theme is continued on a wooden ruler and is used to personalize stationery.*

▼ *Make an album to present your favourite photographs or collection of postcards or scraps.*

6 *Thread the tassels through the loop and pull tightly. Slacken the cord to open the pages.*

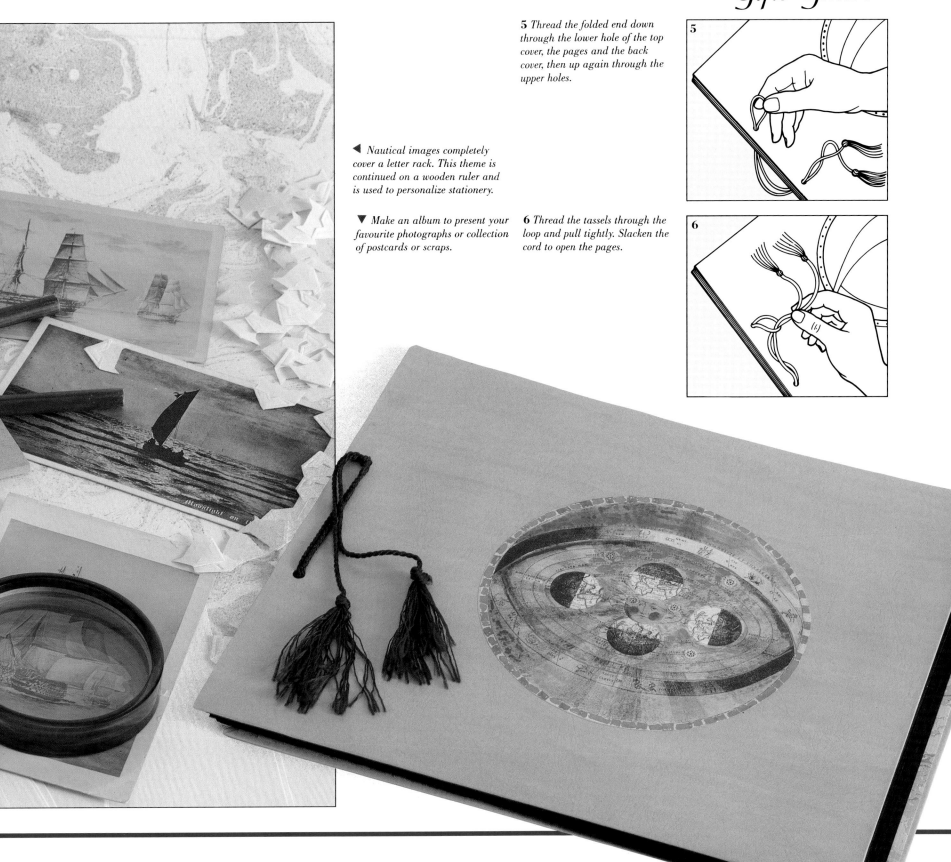

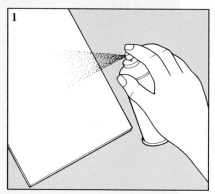

1 *Follow the diagram on page 106 to cut a puppet theatre from mounting board. Cut out the window. Also cut two rectangles of mounting board 40 x 19 cm (16 x 7½ in) for the sides. Spray both sides of the boards with pink spray paint. Lightly spray paint one side of the boards red.*

2 *Choose a giftwrap with a zig-zag design to border the window. As an alternative, you could simply cut your own zig-zag design from coloured paper. Arrange the zig-zag edging around the window on the pink side of the board so that the outer edges meet at the corners. Place a ruler diagonally between two opposite corners and cut through the paper with a craft knife to mitre the corners, cutting outwards from the inner corners. Repeat for each of the other corners.*

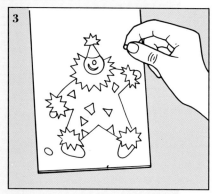

3 *Place the side boards each side of the puppet theatre. Cut clowns, stars and baubles from giftwrap. Place a clown on each side piece within the lower outer corner, then arrange the stars and baubles on the puppet theatre and sides. Stick in place following the gluing technique on page 15.*

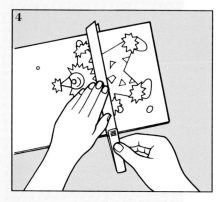

4 *Turn the side pieces over and arrange zig-zags along the upper edges. Place clowns at the lower edges with a few stars and baubles. Stick in place following the gluing technique on page 15. Varnish the theatre pieces with water-based satin varnish following the varnishing technique on page 16 – it is only necessary to varnish the front of the large board. Cut sixteen 20 cm (8 in) lengths of 1.5 cm (⅝ in) wide satin ribbon. Hold one end of two ribbon lengths 10 cm (4 in) above the lower edge of one side piece on the inner long edge, sandwiching the board. Staple in place 5 mm (¼ in) from the edge of the board. Attach two ribbons to the inner long edge 10 cm (4 in) below the upper edge in the same way.*

5 *Attach ribbons to the other side piece, then in corresponding positions to the front theatre piece. Tie the ribbons together in a bow. To make the puppets, roughly cut out animal motifs from giftwrap. Stick to thick card with spray adhesive. Cut around each animal with a craft knife.*

6 *Paint a length of wooden batten and stick to the back of each puppet with wood glue.*

◀ *The triptych style of this colourful puppet theatre means that it will fold away flat when not in use. Amusing puppets are easy to make from animal images stuck to card and are sure to delight your audience.*

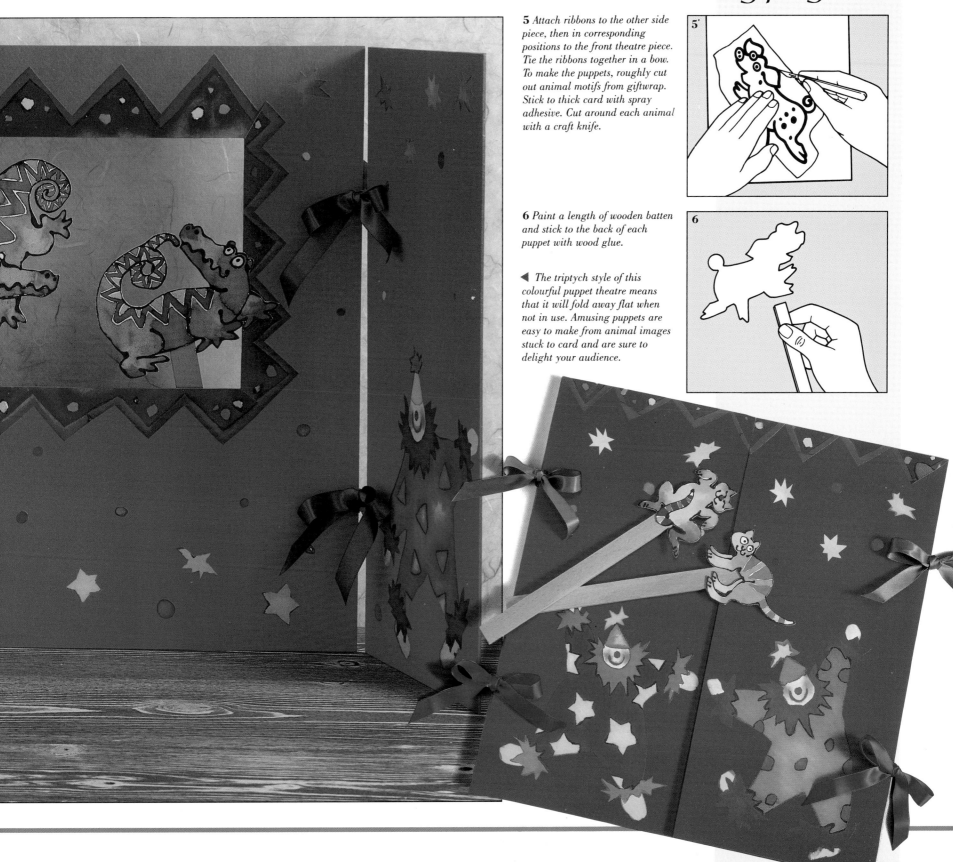

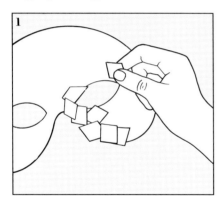

1 *To decorate the silver spirals mask, cut foil sweet wrappers into diamond shapes. Apply PVA medium to a section of the mask and press on a diamond. Coat with PVA medium, then continue applying more diamonds, overlapping the edges until the mask is completely covered.*

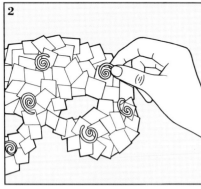

2 *Cut silver foil wrappers lengthwise in half and roll into tight sausage shapes. Bend into spirals. Apply PVA medium to the mask and press on the spirals.*

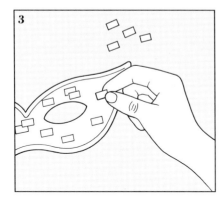

3 *To decorate the small turquoise mask, cover the mask with turquoise foil sweet wrappers, sticking the wrappers in place with PVA medium as before. Cut small rectangles of blue and green foil wrappers and stick to the mask with PVA medium. Decorate the rectangles with silver glitter paint.*

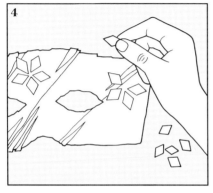

4 *To decorate the mask on a stick, divide the mask diagonally into quarters and cover with blue foil sweet wrappers, applying a different shade to each section and sticking in place with PVA medium. Stick a few strips of contrasting coloured foil onto each section. Cut out diamonds of foil and stick to the mask, arranging the pieces to form flower petals.*

▶ *Plain plastic masks are given an exotic new lease of life with a covering of shiny foil sweet wrappers. Inexpensive masks are available at fancy dress and party shops and can be decorated as simply or as lavishly as you wish.*

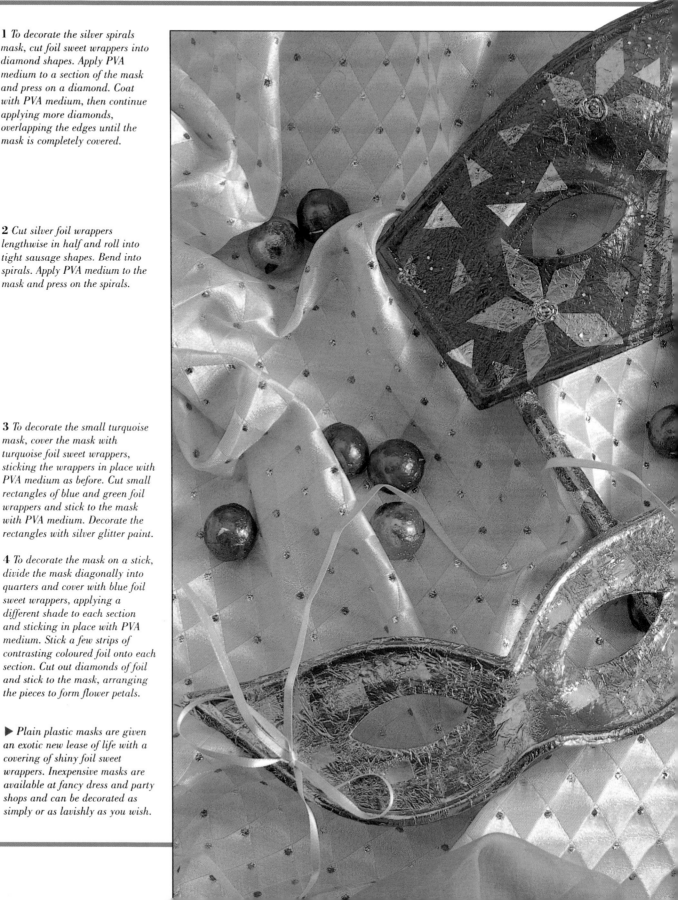

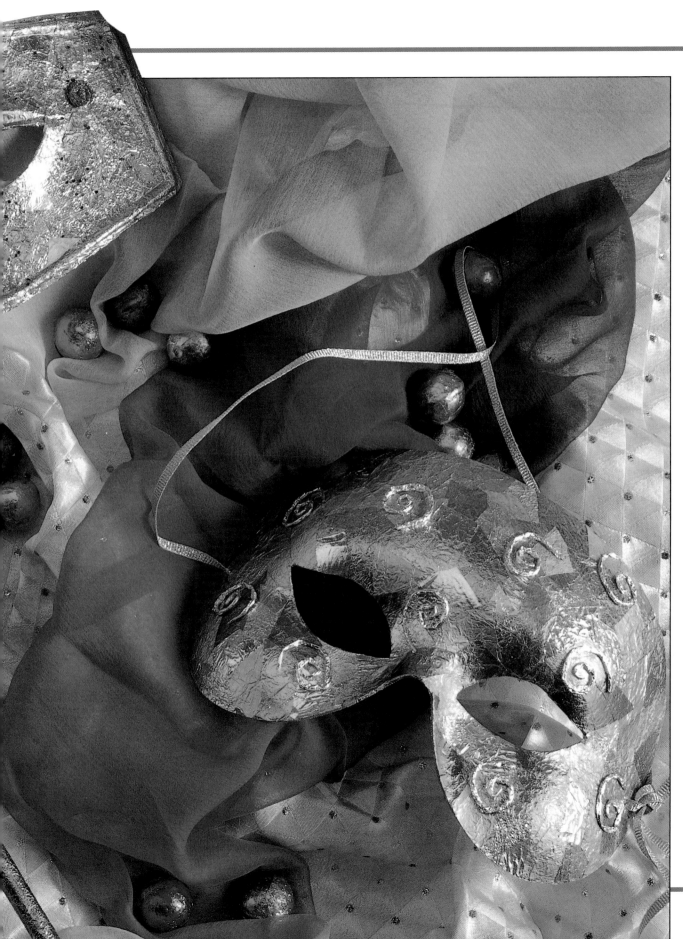

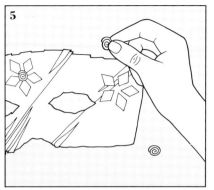

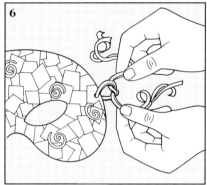

5 *Roll blue foil wrappers into tight sausage shapes and stick to the flower centres. Cover a 35 cm (13½ in) length of wood dowelling with green foil wrappers. Cut and stick triangles of contrasting coloured foil wrappers to the mask and dowelling.*

6 *Trim the outer edges and the eye holes of the masks level. Coat with PVA medium to strengthen the surface and protect the edges. Sprinkle sequin dust, which is the tiny holes cut from sequins, onto the stick mask before the glue dries. Sequin dust is available at specialist bead shops. Leave to dry, then shake off the excess. Stick the length of decorated dowelling behind the mask with strong adhesive. Pierce holes at each side of the other masks and thread with ribbons. Knot the ends behind the holes and fasten the ribbons together. Tie curling silver ribbon to the silver spiral mask.*

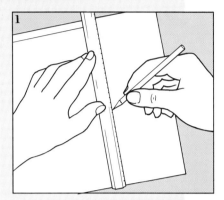

1 Cut a rectangle of mounting board or hardboard 48 x 24.5 cm (19 x 9 ¾ in). Spray paint the board dark red, then lightly spray silver. Paint the cut edges of the board with blue craft paint. Cut strips of giftwrap 1.5 cm (⅝ in) wide to border the checkered squares. Here, a giftwrap illustrated with patterned squares and rectangles was used. Draw a 21.5 cm (8½ in) square onto the centre of the board.

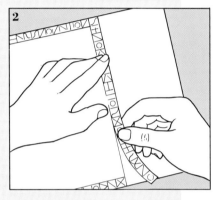

2 Stick the giftwrap strips along the outer edges of the square following the gluing technique on page 15. Trim the ends of the strips to fit. Divide each side of the square into eighths. Join the divisions with a ruler, making 64 small squares. Cut 32 small squares from blue paper.

3 Stick the blue squares in position on alternate drawn squares following the gluing technique on page 15. A small motif, such as the sun shown here, can be stuck in the centre. Cut out motifs from giftwrap and stick to the board at each end of the checkered squares.

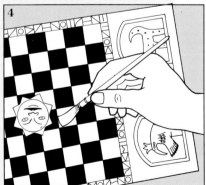

4 Use water-based matt varnish to varnish the board. Crackle glaze the board following the technique on page 17, rubbing white oil paint into the cracks.

▶ Mythical creatures guard this handsome checkers board. The board is easy to construct from mounting board or hardboard.

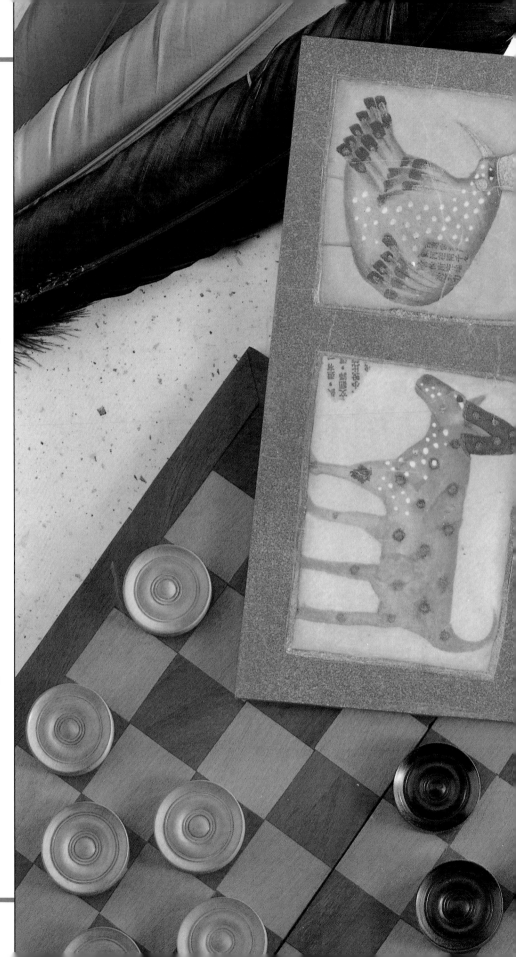

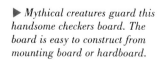

Fabulous Furniture

Even objects as large as furniture will benefit from a decorative découpage touch. Wood veneer papers lend themselves to creating realistic marquetry effects and coloured photocopies can produce entertaining trompe l'oeil illusions.

Fabulous Furniture

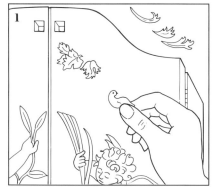

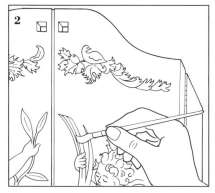

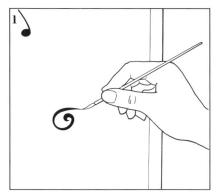

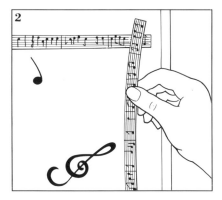

1 *To decorate the corner cupboard, lay the cupboard on its back and remove the handles if possible. Cut out romantic motifs from giftwrap. Arrange the motifs on the cupboard, positioning the largest pieces such as the cherubs used here first. Arrange smaller elements in a row to resemble swags. When you are happy with the design, stick the pieces in place following the gluing technique on page 15.*

2 *Place a box or bottle inside the cupboard to hold the doors slightly open. Varnish the cupboard with water-based matt varnish following the varnishing technique on page 16. Apply only two coats of varnish to the sides of the cupboard and opening edges of the doors. Refer to page 17 to crackle glaze the cupboard, rubbing raw umber oil paint into the cracks. Replace the handles. When the cupbard is hung in position, stick flying cherubs to one with wallpaper border paste.*

1 *To decorate a wooden bedside cupboard, remove the handles first, then sand the surfaces. Apply two coats of white emulsion paint. Leave to dry, then refer to the sponging paint technique on page 14 to sponge the cupboard with beige emulsion paint and silver craft paint. Paint on musical notes and symbols freehand in silver craft paint.*

2 *Cut music staves from a music sheet. Arrange the staves on the door and top of the cupboard in a square or rectangle, overlapping the ends. Place two staves on the drawer. Stick in place following the gluing technique on page 15.*

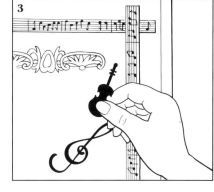

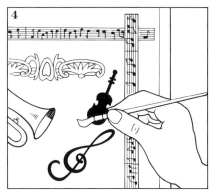

3 Cut borders and musical instruments from giftwrap. Arrange the borders within the music staves and arrange the musical instruments at random. Glue the pieces in place.

4 Varnish the cupboard with water-based satin varnish following the varnishing technique on page 16. Crackle glaze the cupboard, referring to the instructions on page 17 and rubbing oxide yellow oil paint into the cracks. Attach the handles to the cupboard.

◀ Enhance plain wooden cupboards with delicate and nostalgic images to add a feminine and romantic feel to your bedroom furniture.

Fabulous Furniture

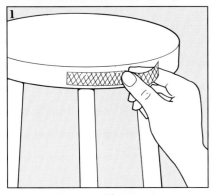

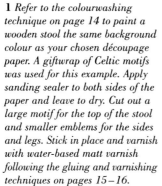

1 *Refer to the colourwashing technique on page 14 to paint a wooden stool the same background colour as your chosen découpage paper. A giftwrap of Celtic motifs was used for this example. Apply sanding sealer to both sides of the paper and leave to dry. Cut out a large motif for the top of the stool and smaller emblems for the sides and legs. Stick in place and varnish with water-based matt varnish following the gluing and varnishing techniques on pages 15–16.*

1 *Choose a giftwrap with a repeat design of muted colours to completely cover an unpainted wooden chair. As a guide, seven sheets of giftwrap were used for this chair. Apply sanding sealer to both sides of the paper and leave to dry. Cut the giftwrap into sections. Starting on the seat, glue the sections in place following the gluing technique on page 15 and overlapping the edges.*

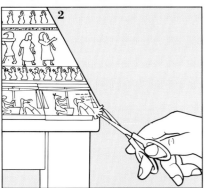

2 *Completely cover the chair, snipping the paper to fit around any corners or curves.*

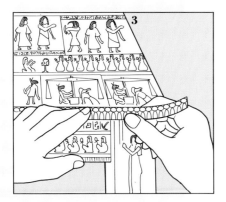

3 *Finish with narrow strips of giftwrap applied along any narrow edges such as the rim of the seat. Varnish the chair with water-based satin varnish following the varnishing technique on page 16. Use polyurethane satin varnish for the last three coats so that the chair is hard-wearing.*

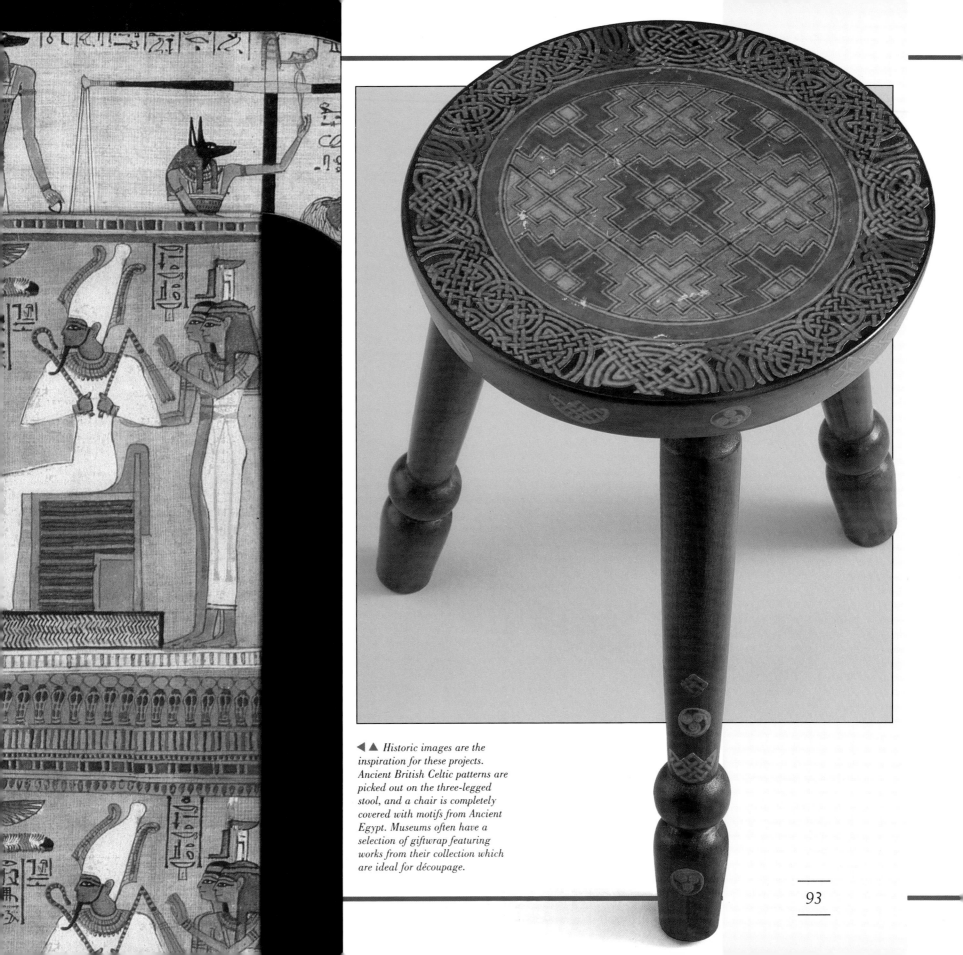

◀ ▲ *Historic images are the inspiration for these projects. Ancient British Celtic patterns are picked out on the three-legged stool, and a chair is completely covered with motifs from Ancient Egypt. Museums often have a selection of giftwrap featuring works from their collection which are ideal for découpage.*

Fabulous Furniture

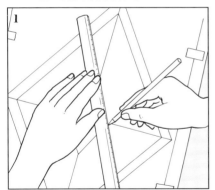

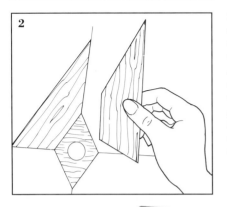

1 *Trace the table top template on page 107 onto tracing paper. You will need wood veneer paper, which is available from specialist paper and art stores, in four colourways. Decide which colour paper you wish to use for each section. Place the tracing face down on the wrong side of the paper and stick in place with masking tape. Redraw along the outlines of one section to transfer it to the paper. Use a ruler for straight lines.*

2 *Transfer all the sections to the relevant coloured papers, then cut out carefully with a craft knife. Cut out the circle in the diamond. Divide the top of the table into quarters with tailor's chalk. Refer to the gluing technique shown on page 15 to stick the diamond in the centre. Stick the circle then the other sections in place, working outwards from the diamond.*

▶ *Wood veneer papers are cunningly used to achieve this realistic marquetry effect on a wooden table top.*

3 *Rub off the chalk marks. To make a decorative edging, cut the papers into strips slightly narrower than the depth of the table top. Cut diagonally into sections approximately 3.5 cm (1½ in) long. Mark the centre of each edge of the table top. Cut one of the diagonal sections into a triangle for each side and glue to the centre. Glue the diagonal sections along the edge each side of the triangle. Trim the last sections.*

4 *Cut a diamond of paper and glue centrally to each support strut. Follow the varnishing technique shown on page 16 to varnish the table with eight coats of water-based matt varnish. Finish with two coats of matt polyurethane varnish, which will mellow the colouring of the découpage and make the table top more hard-wearing.*

Fabulous Furniture

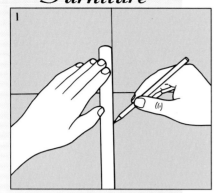

1 *To make a patchwork screen, collect scraps of colourful giftwraps and magazine pages. Cut into 7.5 cm (3 in) squares. Divide each face of the screen into quarters with a pencil.*

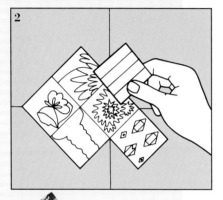

2 *With the screen laying open flat on a floor, arrange the squares positioned diagonally on top. Keep similar coloured squares side by side, gradually changing the colour scheme as you work across the screen.*

▶ *A patchwork of stunning colour covers this majestic screen. Although time-consuming to do, the method is very simple and you will have a lasting heirloom to treasure when the screen is finished.*

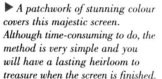

3 *When you are happy with the colour scheme, stick the squares in place, starting at the centre and working outwards along the divisions and following the gluing technique on page 15. Trim the outer squares with a craft knife to fit. Apply five coats of water-based satin varnish.*

1 *To decorate the pink screen, paint the screen sections with pink emulsion paint. Follow the sponging paint technique on page 14 to sponge on cerise pink emulsion paint. Leave to dry. Cut out motifs from giftwrap and arrange across the top of each section, sticking the motifs in place with masking tape. Follow the gluing technique on page 15 to stick the motifs in place, then apply five coats of water-based matt varnish.*

▼ *A simple arrangement of pastel motifs makes this elegant screen an easy project to recreate.*

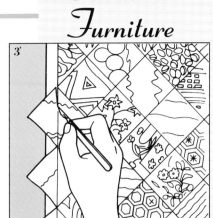

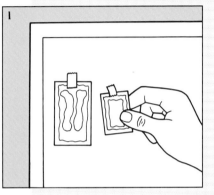

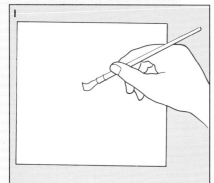

1 *You can photograph your own still-life arrangement overhead or use photographic images from catalogues or magazines. Make a colour photocopy of the image and enlarge it to a suitable size. As a guide for enlarging on a photocopier, decide upon the width of image you want to end up with, preferably measured in millimetres, for example 270 mm. Measure the width of the image to be enlarged, for example 94 cm. Divide the first measurement by the second. The photocopy should be enlarged to the resulting number as a percentage, for example 287%. Apply sanding sealer to both sides of the photocopy.*

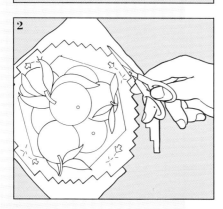

2 *Leave to dry, then cut out around the image.*

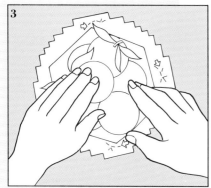

3 *Arrange the image on the table top. Stick in place following the gluing technique on page 15.*

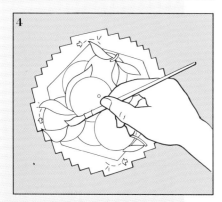

4 *Varnish the table top with water-based matt varnish following the varnishing technique shown on page 16.*

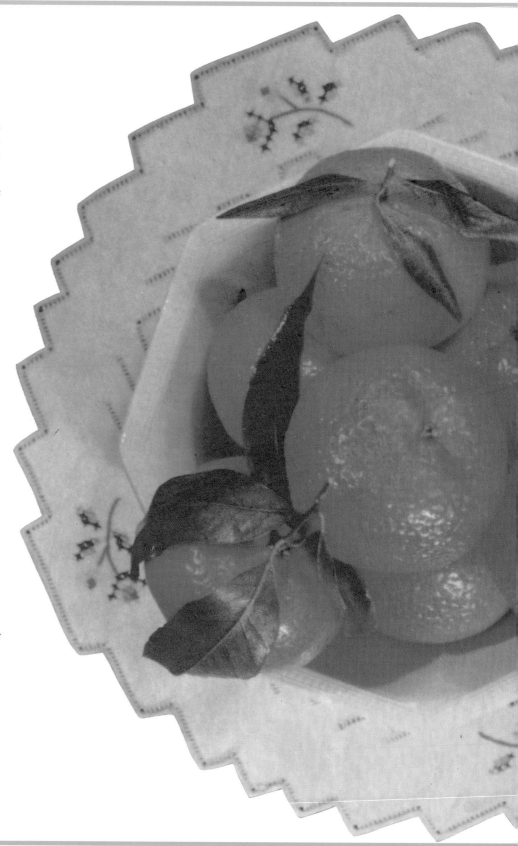

▶ *Guests will look twice at this colourful side table with its trompe l'oeil of a bowl of sumptuous clementines.*

Fabulous Furniture

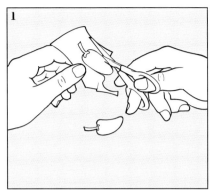

1 *Thin yellow and apricot craft paints with water. Refer to the colourwashing technique on page 14 to paint a small chest, blending the colours together. Cut out motifs from giftwrap or magazines. Photographic images of foods and flowers were used to decorate this chest.*

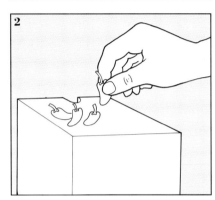

2 *With the drawer fronts uppermost, arrange the motifs on the fronts, grouping together similar images on each drawer.*

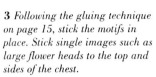

◀ *An ideal storage chest for the kitchen, this small chest of drawers is decorated with inspiring and exotic foodstuffs.*

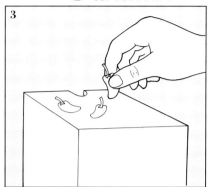

3 *Following the gluing technique on page 15, stick the motifs in place. Stick single images such as large flower heads to the top and sides of the chest.*

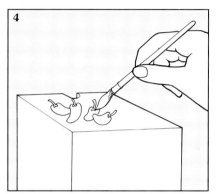

4 *Varnish the decorated chest with water-based satin varnish following the varnishing technique shown on page 16. You need apply only one coat of varnish to the sides of the drawers.*

Fabulous Furniture

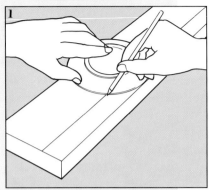

1 *You will need a length of 2.5 cm (1 in) thick prepared planed timber 20 cm (8 in) longer than your window and 15 cm (6 in) wide. With a pencil and ruler, draw a line lengthwise on the wood 10 cm (4 in) below the upper long edge to mark the depth of the pelmet. Place an upturned saucer on the centre of the wood, the circumference against the lower edge. Draw around the lower section of the saucer.*

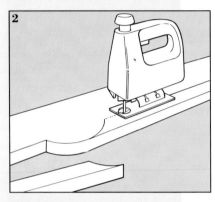

2 *Using a power-driven jigsaw or handcoping saw, cut along the length of the ruled line to the circle edge. Repeat, starting from the other end of the pelmet. Next, cut around the circle edge, working outwards from the bottom of the curve.*

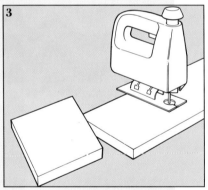

3 *Cut two 10 cm (4 in) squares of 2.5 cm (1 in) thick prepared planed timber for the side pieces.*

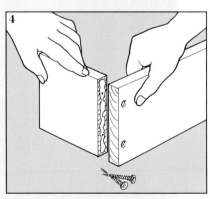

4 *To join the side pieces at right angles to the pelmet, drill screw holes through the front of the pelmet into the cut ends of the side pieces. Countersink the holes on the front of the pelmet to allow for filling. Spread wood glue on the drilled ends of the side pieces, wipe off the excess. Screw the pieces together. Leave to dry.*

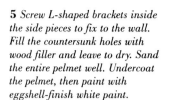

5 *Screw L-shaped brackets inside the side pieces to fix to the wall. Fill the countersunk holes with wood filler and leave to dry. Sand the entire pelmet well. Undercoat the pelmet, then paint with eggshell-finish white paint.*

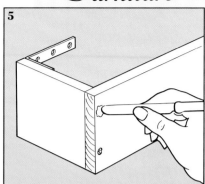

◄ ▼ *Classical pictures in black and white are découpaged onto a shaped wooden pelmet to border a pretty window. A chunky knob to hold back the curtain provides a matching detail.*

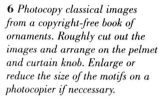

6 *Photocopy classical images from a copyright-free book of ornaments. Roughly cut out the images and arrange on the pelmet and curtain knob. Enlarge or reduce the size of the motifs on a photocopier if neccessary.*

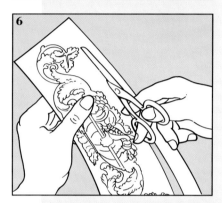

7 *Apply sanding sealer to both sides of the paper. Cut out around the motifs.*

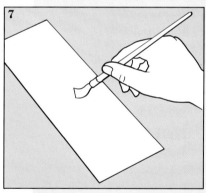

8 *Glue the motifs in place. Follow the gluing and varnishing techniques on pages 15–16 to varnish them with water-based satin varnish .*

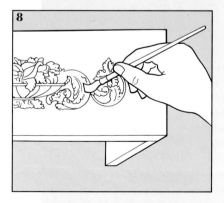

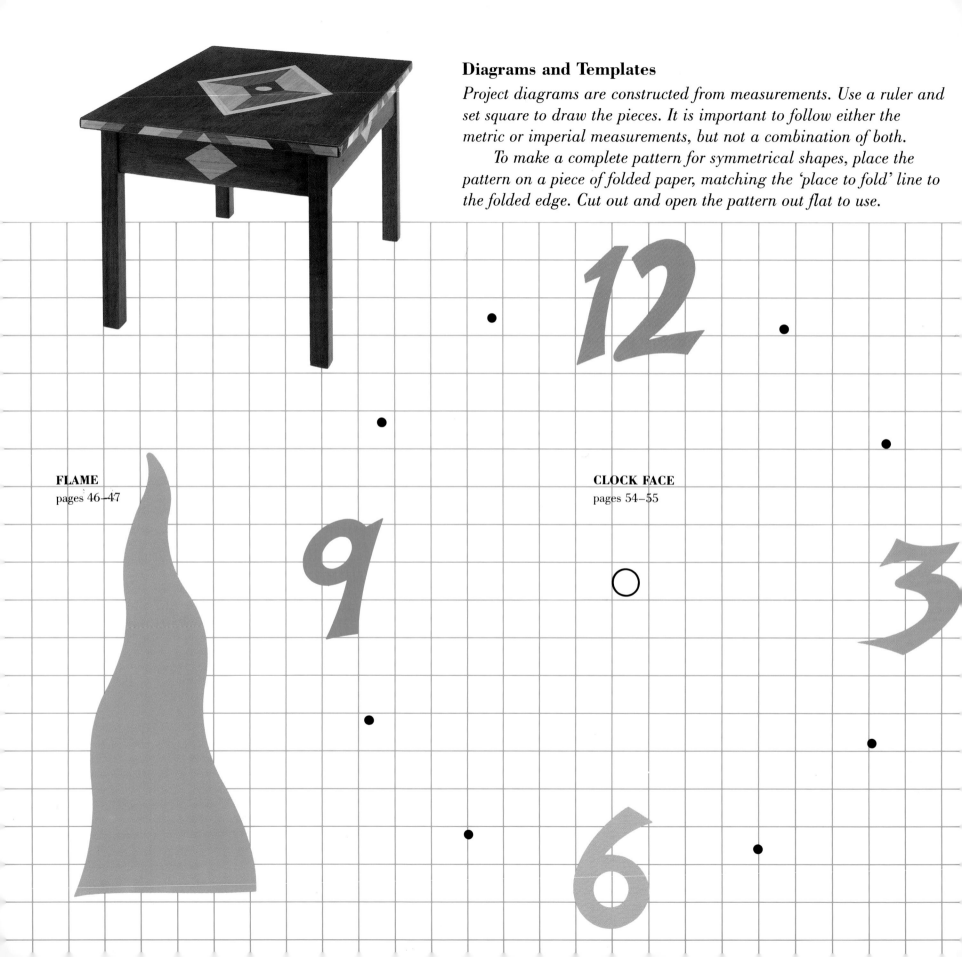

Diagrams and Templates

Project diagrams are constructed from measurements. Use a ruler and set square to draw the pieces. It is important to follow either the metric or imperial measurements, but not a combination of both.

To make a complete pattern for symmetrical shapes, place the pattern on a piece of folded paper, matching the 'place to fold' line to the folded edge. Cut out and open the pattern out flat to use.

FLAME
pages 46–47

CLOCK FACE
pages 54–55

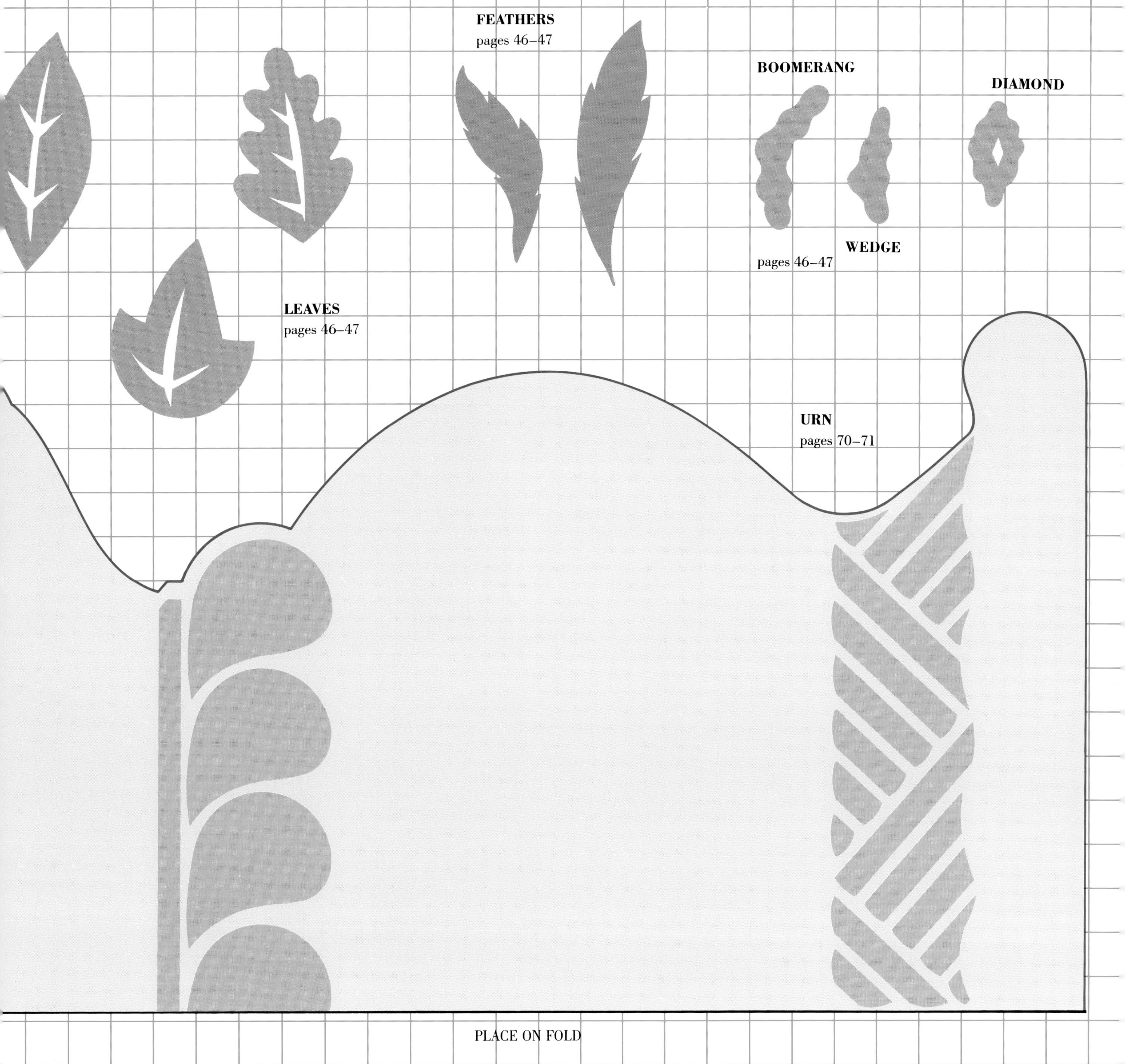

FEATHERS
pages 46–47

BOOMERANG

DIAMOND

WEDGE

pages 46–47

LEAVES
pages 46–47

URN
pages 70–71

PLACE ON FOLD

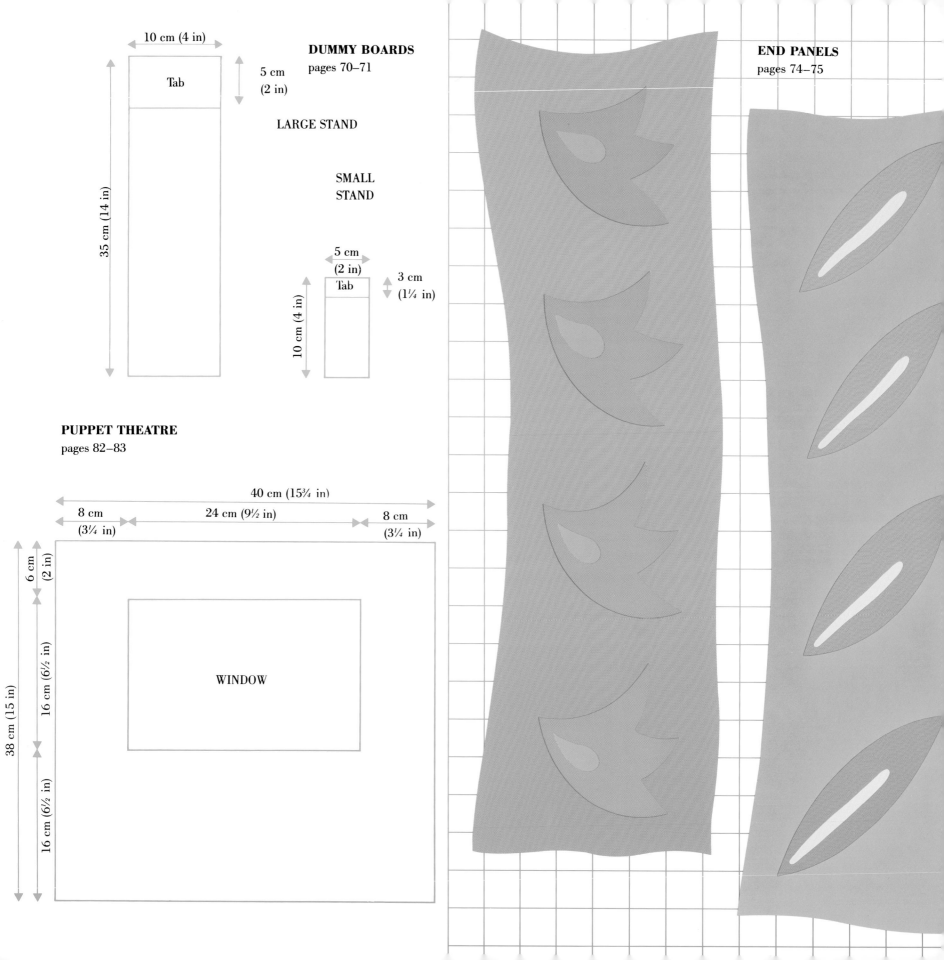

DUMMY BOARDS
pages 70–71

10 cm (4 in)

5 cm (2 in)

Tab

LARGE STAND

35 cm (14 in)

SMALL STAND

5 cm (2 in)

3 cm (1¼ in)

Tab

10 cm (4 in)

PUPPET THEATRE
pages 82–83

40 cm (15¾ in)

8 cm (3¼ in)

24 cm (9½ in)

8 cm (3¼ in)

6 cm (2 in)

16 cm (6½ in)

WINDOW

38 cm (15 in)

16 cm (6½ in)

16 cm (6½ in)

END PANELS
pages 74–75

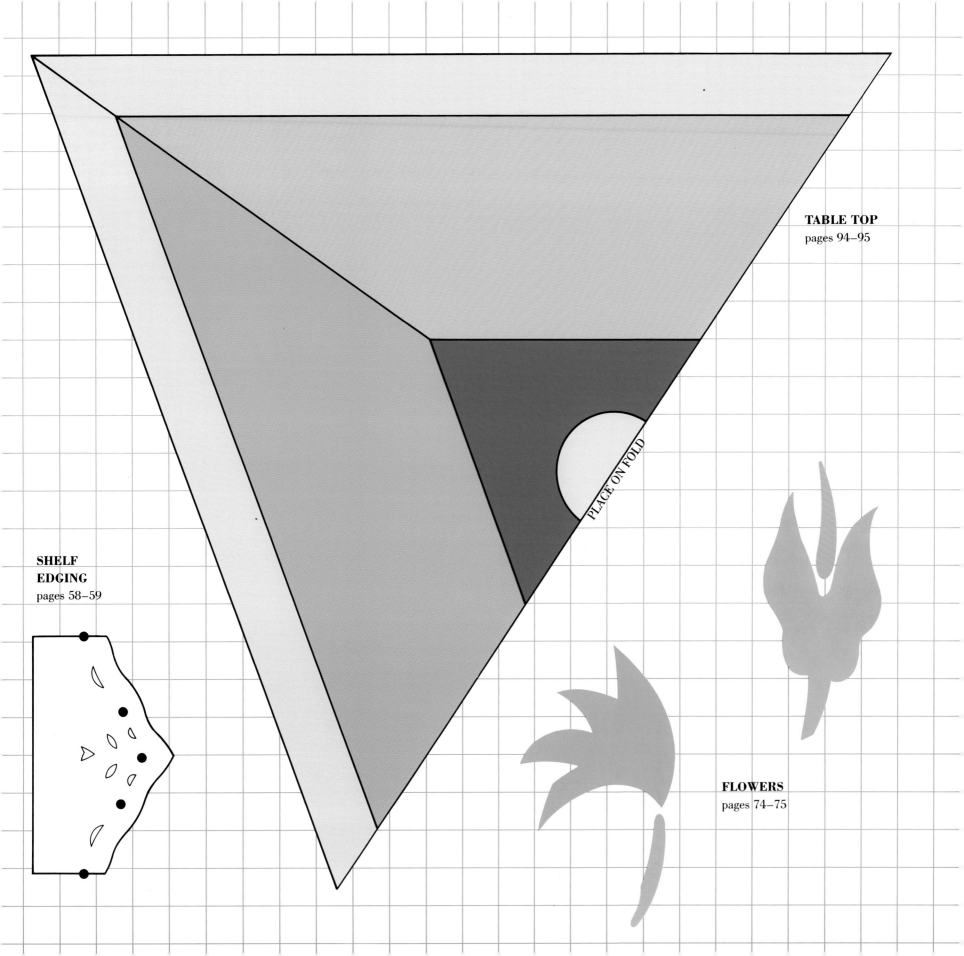

TABLE TOP
pages 94–95

PLACE ON FOLD

**SHELF
EDGING**
pages 58–59

FLOWERS
pages 74–75

Managing Editor: Jo Finnis

Editor: Adèle Hayward

Designer: Phil Gorton

Photography: Steve Tanner

Photographic Direction: Phil Gorton

Illustrations: Geoff Denney Associates

Typesetting: Elaine Morris

Production: Ruth Arthur; Sally Connolly;

Neil Randles; Karen Staff; Jonathan Tickner

Director of Production: Gerald Hughes